CHAMPAGNE LADIES

Effervescent at Any Age

DR. SUSAN R. MEYER

Published: March 2026

Paperback ISBN: 979-8-9951103-1-6
Hardcover: ISBN: 979-8- 9951103-2-3
Library of Congress Number: 2026906620

For information address:
The Three Tomatoes Book Publishing
6 Soundview Rd.
Glen Cove, NY 11542

Cover design: Susan Herbst
Interior design: Susan Herbst
Author Photo: Anne Akers & Sharon Marantz Walsh

Disclaimer: The stories and perspectives in this book are drawn from interviews conducted by Dr. Susan R. Meyer. While the women's experiences are represented faithfully, some details have been condensed or reordered for clarity.

*Dedicated to all the Champagne Ladies,
especially The Three Tomatoes members,
and my grandmother, Kathryn Meyer
and my aunt, Lynn Meyer.*

THE ORIGINAL CHAMPAGNE LADY

BARBE NICOLE PONSARDIN WAS BORN on December 16, 1777, in Reims, France, and died July 29, 1866, in Boursault, France, at eighty-nine. She married François Clicquot in 1798, who died seven years later. A widow at twenty-seven, she became known as *La Veuve Clicquot* — **the Widow Clicquot**. This allowed her to take over their vineyard at a time when women were prohibited from owning businesses. The addition of veuve to her name allowed her to circumvent these restrictions.

Madam Clicquot fought to distribute her wines. She managed to continue despite wars and plague. She experimented and experimented to create a quality product. She created a process called ridding to remove sediment from the wine. She also created a special sparkling wine by leaving the skins in the mix and became a mastermind behind the creation of sparkling rosé wine. Her champagne is still highly valued today.

Both in age and boldness, the widow Clicquot—Veuve Clicquot—was truly a Champagne Lady and an inspiration to us all.

FOREWORD

BUCKLE UP YOUR SEATBELTS—YOUR ideas about what "old" looks like are about to be delightfully upended. Dr. Susan R. Meyer has interviewed thirty-eight women who are redefining life in their sixties, seventies, eighties, and even nineties.

These are women who came of age in the 1950s, 1960s, and 1970s—decades that reshaped what women could do, dream, and become. They remember when a woman couldn't get a credit card without a male cosigner (thank you, Bella Abzug, for helping change that in 1974 with the Equal Credit Opportunity Act). They cheered *Roe v. Wade.* They pushed open the doors to the corner office, and if it didn't open, they became their own boss. They tossed aside the pearls-and-sweater "Mom" archetypes they grew up with on TV and celebrated every time Mary Tyler Moore threw her hat in the air.

They fought the "isms" of their time—sexism, racism, antisemitism—and now they're kicking the last "acceptable ism" to the curb—ageism.

Susan has championed these women in her book *Fifty Over*

Fifty: Wise and Wild Women Creating Wonderful Lives (and You Can Too!), and now again as she revisits some of those voices and introduces new ones she admires. I'm honored to appear in both books—and honored to be her publisher for this one.

I've known Susan for many years—don't ask how many, because at my age they all blur together and everything feels like it happened yesterday... or maybe five years ago. I believe we first met at a roundtable luncheon hosted by our mutual friend Randie Levine Miller, who loved gathering interesting women who didn't yet know each other.

When it came time for introductions, Susan stood out. She was brief about herself and far more interested in asking thoughtful questions of the other women. And when Susan asks a question, she truly listens. She absorbs the answer, asks a followup, and if she hears even a hint of hesitation about someone's next chapter, she's right there with encouragement. That is her superpower—and it's what makes these thirty-eight stories so compelling, inspiring, and wonderfully human.

Thank you, Susan, from all of us, for being a supportive friend, a gentle buttkicker, and a champion of women stepping boldly into their tomorrows.

Bette Davis famously said, "Growing old ain't for sissies." Well, let me assure you—there are no sissies in this book.

Cheryl Benton
The Three Tomatoes

CHAMPAGNE POETRY

CATCHING THE MOMENT
Elizabeth Fowler Sullivan

I'm catching the moment and stashing it away
from the hands of a clock that doesn't want it to stay.
I'm hanging on to a feeling and I simply refuse
to let Time take from me what I don't want to lose;
Out of nowhere it happened, this serendipity!
Out of nothing something came, especially for me.
And from somewhere, just like magic, I suddenly could see;
I must somehow find a way to always be;

Catching the moment and stashing it away
from the hands of a clock that doesn't want it to stay.
I'm hanging on to a feeling and I simply refuse
to let Time take from me what I don't want to lose;
Out of nowhere it happened, this serendipity!
Out of nothing something came, especially for me.
And from somewhere, just like magic, I suddenly could see;
I must somehow find a way to always be;

Catching the moment, stashing it away,
  catching the moment!

Elizabeth Sullivan, 95, contributed this poem from the wonderful collection on her website. The mother of five musicians, she

writes poems or lyrics every day. She is also a singer, appearing often with her daughters. She and KT and Heather perform regularly on cruise ships.

INTRODUCTION
Why this book, why now?

THERE ARE SO MANY AMAZING women who inspire me. More than a decade ago, I had written about some of these women in a book, *Fifty over Fifty: Wise and Wild Women Creating Wonderful Lives (and You Can Too!)*. I had given it little thought until I began to hear about the impact of that book. A coach told me that being included was a huge honor and self-esteem builder for her and for the other women she had recommended for the project. She also told me that she gives a copy to every woman she coaches. I knew then that there were still women who needed to be honored and women who needed to be reached.

The ever-increasing number of older women in visible roles had led me to hope that we were finally moving beyond the notion of the withered crone, past her expiration date, sitting in a rocking chair or staring blankly from a wheelchair in the lounge of a nursing home. Yet, in a discussion of this project, a former studio head, whom I respect, said that it must be hard for women to reach an age where they no longer turn heads.

It brought me right back to the still widely held notion that a woman's primary purpose was reproduction and caregiving—that her sole reason for being attractive was using her allure to attract a mate. The late Barbara Sher, noted career coach, said that nature, caring only about the continuation of the species, no longer paid any attention to menopausal women. Sher posited that this gives them greater freedom, under the cloak of invisibility, to become who they want to be.

For Boomers and the last of the pre-Boomers, the evil twins—gender discrimination and age discrimination—remain our companions, all the more evident as more and more women come into their full power. We remember job listings separated by gender. We dealt with being told that certain careers were "not for women." We remember the other executives flying first class while we flew coach, being paid significantly less than men in the same role because, we were told, we didn't have families to provide for, and being barred from meeting in gender-restricted clubs. One of the women I interviewed told me that she was forced to sit on the floor in the hall of a country club instead of sitting in the dining room (where she was supposed to chair a meeting) because women were not permitted inside. We adhered to limiting rules about appropriate behavior and to dress codes.

Despite these barriers and restrictions—negative views about the value, worth, and acceptable roles for women—we entered adulthood with a dazzling yet often confusing array of possibilities. We were the first women to enter careers formerly reserved for men. We were confrontational. We fought loudly for what we wanted and needed. Often, we created new kinds of careers and countless woman-owned businesses. We expect more of life, and many of us don't view aging as the enemy or as a limitation.

Stephanie Raffelock, in *Creatrix Rising: Unlocking the Power of Midlife Women*, reminds us that Crone, the descriptor for women at midlife and beyond, is a negative term, suggesting decay and rot. Instead, she writes of the Creatrix. You will find ample evidence of this archetype in action in these pages.

All this gave me hope for the future of women. I started this book sure that the stories of women, and resilience and joy, would remind other women in their mid-sixties through well over seventy that we are still of great value. Much has happened to make me realize that this is also written for younger women, who will once more have to fight some of the same battles we were fighting in our twenties.

I went through the first part of my reproductive years with limited access to birth control and none to legal abortion. We fought for our right to value our appearance; however we chose to present ourselves to the world, to not be treated as meat or decorative objects, and to feel safe walking alone. We fought to keep Planned Parenthood open. We sought to avoid the back room or—worse still—the coat hanger abortions my grandmother endured. We fought for salary equality, decrying the notion that men should be paid more because they had families. We championed the ERA.

Younger women are coming into a labor market where, although the margin has decreased by a few cents, salary equality still remains a battle. Gender and age discrimination are still widespread, with many women faced with both. The ERA has yet to be added to the Constitution. The Supreme Court overturned the fifty-year-old Roe v Wade decision that legalized abortion.

And now, a few words from Matt Birk, 2022 candidate for Lieutenant Governor of Minnesota: "It's not over. Our culture loudly, but also stealthily, promotes abortion. Telling women they should look a certain way, have careers, all these things. You know, women used to not be able to vote in our country. Now we let 'em drive."

I'm pretty sure that he's not alone in this "keep them barefoot, pregnant, and keeping house for us men" viewpoint. Thank you, Matt, for reminding us of who some people still think we are.

So, I hope that this book will also encourage younger women not only to battle on but also to be encouraged by older women who managed to succeed, create, and enjoy life despite—or perhaps because of—all the barriers.

When we look, it's easy to see that we are surrounded by older women with interesting, and often untold, stories. And, like fine wine, these women often keep improving with age. These strong, resilient women fascinate me. Over the past two years, the researcher in me quietly collected stories around a few central notions that I wanted to examine.

I wondered what makes us remain resilient. Why do some women bounce back, remain buoyant, and keep growing? Is it possible to keep bouncing back? How many times is it possible to come back? Do we come back to the same level or lose a certain degree of resilience each time, and at some point stop bouncing back at all? What makes certain women so vibrantly alive? What sustains their joy, their curiosity, their sense of purpose?

To explore these questions, I returned to the women from my earlier work—reinterviewing several of the fifty women whose lives had already shaped my thinking—and expanded the circle. In total, more than thirty-eight women between the ages of sixty-six and ninety-seven opened their lives to me. They shared not only their histories, but the inner architecture of their resilience: the choices, habits, beliefs, and relationships that have allowed them to keep growing rather than shrinking with age.

I bring to this project my own life experience and a passion for motivating women to be visible. I also bring decades of coaching, studying adult development, and an addiction to collecting life stories, including those in my doctoral dissertation in the mid-80s.

My role was to listen, interpret, and weave their lived wisdom with what research tells us about vitality, meaning, and emotional longevity. I have so many questions—are there common traits, patterns of thinking, ways of loving, or daily practices that help women stay lit from within? What can the rest of us learn from them?

In *Fifty Over Fifty: Wise and Wild Women Creating Wonderful Lives (And You Can Too!)*, I identified the seven factors as contributing to a life well lived. In these interviews, an eighth emerged. These serve as the framework for this book, clustered around the core factor of resilience.

1. **Resilience:** It's the power or ability to recover from adversity; elasticity; buoyancy. It should not be seen as "bouncing back," as some older definitions suggest, but rather learning and adapting to move forward. We will all face challenges in life—disappointment, disease, loss—all of these can stop us in our tracks. Sometimes, so much seems to be going wrong that it's hard to resist the urge to take to our beds... forever. After all, it worked for Victorian ladies, didn't it? However, if you are going to rise above your challenges and thrive, you will need the ability to find alternate paths through or around them.
   Dr. Eli Ginzberg saw seven components of resilience: Competence, Confidence, Connection, Character, Contribution, Coping, and Control. As Dr. Ann Clancy points out, resilience has been redefined as part of a life that is always moving forward. There is no "bouncing back."
2. **Persistence** is lasting or enduring tenacity; persevering despite obstacles, opposition, and discouragement. If something did not work the first time, these women tried again, made adjustments, and tried yet again. They didn't give up or walk away

from what they knew they wanted. Neither did they maintain a false optimism, chasing after something that could never become a reality. Instead, these persistent women identified the core elements of what they wanted and explored other paths to meet their needs.

3. **Curiosity, Restlessness, and Openness to New Things** involve exploration, investigation, and learning. Curious people have a thirst for knowledge, and often, a sort of restlessness. They might be unable to resist either a new challenge or something different to explore. So many of these women are lifelong learners. They are always exploring; some described themselves as easily bored. Closely related is curiosity. This also includes a sense of adventure. Women who create their ideal lives are much more likely to say, "Why not?" than "Why?" If offered the opportunity to create a new business or take to the open road, they say, "Yes."

4. **Bricolage:** This is a term that has long fascinated me. Bricolage has been defined as taking objects that have been used before and reorganizing them within a new perspective. The process is ongoing. The women I spoke with continued to develop, to refine, to grow, and change throughout their lives. They continue to contribute because they have a strong sense of purpose, a mission. They have a passion for living a full life and for what they do.

   Many of the most successful women I spoke with were able to scan the horizon and see emerging trends and possibilities. They also found ways to use skills learned in seemingly very different fields in new ways. This requires being able to take both a broad and a narrow view. It is easier to create your ideal life when you see how everything you know and have done can be recombined and synthesized, reused in unexpected ways, or brought together in an unusual manner.

5. **Dealing with Fear:** We are all afraid sometimes. We are, in fact, hard-wired to sense danger and flee. Unfortunately, our brains often remain in cave-dweller mode, conditioned to revert immediately to flight or hiding as the only options. Women who thrive learn how to handle fear differently. Yes, they feel fear, but they work through it. They face difficult situations head on. They separate unrealistic fears from realistic ones and then develop a plan to move beyond fear and into action.

6. **Creating a Legacy and Having Fun:** While it is easy to think of legacy as a financial issue, that definition is very narrow. Legacy can also be something transmitted by or received from an ancestor or predecessor. It could be a book you have written, an organization you have created, or that secret recipe handed down from your grandmother. I've added the notion of having fun to this definition, since this seemed to be a key element in how these women thought about their lives. Having fun and giving back were inextricably linked for them.

7. **Connection:** The theme of connection and community underscores everything I heard in the interviews. Friendships, family, and groups were recurring themes that don't fit neatly into any of the other categories, yet are part of the life of every woman I interviewed, as well as part of my own life.

When the pandemic hit, and New Yorkers went into lockdown, Cheryl Benton thought about the single women who were part of her Three Tomatoes community and started a virtual cocktail hour where women could have a sense of connection, get support, laugh, and share video and book recommendations. Years later, the group still meets, and although some drop in less frequently, strong friendships have been created.

I'm part of a trio of sorority sisters who met in the sixties and have shared triumphs and tragedies, despite distance and very different interests and lifestyles over the decades. Even though we have become a duet, I still feel our third sister with us.

At eighty years old, I feel that I'm coming into my own in a different way. As aging improves champagne—it needs at least three years to be considered vintage—my ideas have deepened and become richer. I'm revisiting what I learned from fifty women over fifty—including myself—to see if the characteristics that made us vibrant then are still at the core of women years later.

This book is a collection of stories, based on my interviews. I invite you to think of them as chats or glimpses into another's life, and I hope they inspire you the way they have inspired me. Relax, curl up with your favorite beverage, eavesdrop, and reflect on your own life. Where do you see yourself in these stories? What will you take away from this to bring out the Champagne Lady within you?

PREFACE

I can't resist interviewing every interesting woman that I meet;
they're all fascinating, they're all Champagne Ladies.
~Susan R. Meyer

I'VE BEEN WRITING AND TEACHING most of my life. When my mother became ill—I was somewhere around seven or eight—I stayed with her parents for a few weeks and began to write a newsletter about what was going on. By the time I was ten, I was lining up all my dolls and teaching them. These two threads—writing and teaching—remained intertwined and transformed into writing and coaching.

I had a rocky childhood. My mother died when I was nine. For a while, my two-year-old brother and I went to live with my father's brother and his family; my father remarried, and I spent a few years with a stereotypical wicked stepmother who eventually arranged for me to move across the country to live with my grandmother and alcoholic grandfather when I was thirteen. Reading everything I could get my hands on and writing were my refuges.

In high school, I avoided learning Algebra by writing very bad poetry during class. The full impact of this lack of poetic ability was brought home when my grandmother found the poems and, thinking she was doing a wonderful thing, typed them all up. I'll spare the world the one fragment I remember.

My grandparents wrote articles on tropical fish. A great aunt was a novelist and political writer. My parents, who met in high school, both wrote for the high school magazine. My father became a technical writer for a couple of McGraw Hill publications. At one point, I found my mother's diaries—full of character sketches, humor, and a fair amount of sarcasm. So, I came to writing naturally.

It took a long time, though, to realize what I wanted to write about. For years, my outlet was curriculum development. Then, I developed a career planning course that focused on life histories and discovered many unforgettable women. That got me fascinated with life histories; I decided that I needed a doctorate to research and write about women, so I investigated Teachers College, Columbia. As I looked at the program more closely, I realized that it was the perfect field to bring together my interests in writing, counseling, and teaching.

Many of the people I met there became influences in my future career. It got me interested in transformative learning and how women grew and changed through lives. I was employed at Medgar Evers College. At that time, it had a large Black, female, older population. I was teaching in a program that combined internships with career development courses, so my first major writing effort was a dissertation that was based on interviews about changing self-esteem with women who had entered college after a long absence from education.

When the funding for the program ended, I discovered Civil Service and had several staff development and training positions within NYC agencies, eventually moving to the Transit Authority. At 50, I left Transit with no plan. I spent a lot of time bouncing around, trying to figure out who I was and how I could do what called to me so strongly.

I eventually developed a coaching practice. I realized that I most wanted to coach women who needed a sense of direction and a healthy sense of self, and I created a program for underserved women that was highly successful – 90% of the graduates either had jobs or returned to school when they completed the program. Years later, that program became the basis for *I'm Susan and I'm a Serial Careerist*, published by The Three Tomatoes.

Of course, the funding for the program ended, and I couldn't figure out how to market it. I continued to coach, wrote a little bit, and sort of stumbled along for a while until I realized that I wasn't really writing. Blogging got me started writing again.

I was once again called to write about women's lives, so I wrote *50 Over 50: Wise and Wild Women Creating Wonderful Lives (And You Can Too!)* It combined stories with coaching suggestions. I missed, though, being able to use the whole interviews.

I continued coaching through a coaching company, still thinking about those interviews. Becoming more active in The Three Tomatoes meant that I was meeting a constant stream of amazing women. How could I not start doing interviews?

Champagne Ladies grew out of that need to give women a space for longer stories and find the ones that would inspire other women and remind us all that we can be valuable and interesting and – yes – like good champagne, effervescent as long as we live.

TABLE OF CONTENTS

Part 1

COACHES AND AUTHORS

I NTERVIEWED A LARGE GROUP of coaches for this book because I was curious about how the lives of women who help others change had changed over time. How did their experiences shape professional decisions and practices? How did they continue to build meaningful lives and deal with obstacles?

Each of these women is an excellent coach and a prolific communicator, authoring books, newsletters, blogs, and columns. Deb Roth is a consistent video presence, conducting monthly New Moon circles and other programs, and Beatty Cohan has a radio show. Donna Karlin has been extremely prolific and has a catalog of books too long to list here. Minx Boren writes daily. Her work includes poetry, blog posts, and books.

Each has created a different coaching practice and has changed and adapted their practice to fit the times and their needs. Within all their stories, you will find resilience, persistence, curiosity, bricolage, and an openness to new things.

Deb reminds me that, as we age and grow, we seek deeper

meaning. You will see how spirituality, over time, becomes central to her practice. She gained confidence in her true path as she moved forward and modified her practice to more clearly reflect her passion.

Beatty displays the special kind of resilience that led her to take on challenges like growing from unknown outsider to tennis champion. She relied on resilience and especially the ability to adapt to her changing circumstances.

As you follow Minx's journey, you will see bricolage as she builds on, recombines, and synthesizes cooking, health, and wellness into health-wise coaching.

Donna's path was strongly influenced by changing life circumstances. She is extraordinarily resilient and another example of bricolage, as she built on each experience based on what she learned.

Note that both Minx and Donna exemplify resilience as redefined in the first chapter. In the face of multiple difficulties, they examined the current situation, drew on their knowledge and resources, redefined the context, held a positive mindset, and created a new path.

Diane DiResta focuses on public speaking and executive presence. In 1993, she self-published her book *Knockout Presentations*, now in its third edition, followed by *Give Fear the Finger* in 2014.

Rita J. Battat is the co-author of the independent publishers award-winning book, *Replacement Children: The Unconscious Script*. She has worn many hats, working as a talent manager and freelance literary agent. Rita continues to work as a life coach with over 40 years of experience.

MINX BOREN
Health Wise and Heart-Forward

*I've spent a lifetime researching what it means to be healthy
and health-wise. If I'm looking, the answers show up.
Then I reach out and ask—How can I use this?
What do I need to know? What can I do with this?*

MINX IS A COACH, AUTHOR, and poet whose life's work is an unfolding mosaic of healing, cooking, teaching, and soulful inquiry. She's spent decades asking questions, listening for the answers, and building creative, joyful solutions—especially during life's toughest chapters. Minx grew up in the restaurant world and studied food from around the world, including traveling with her uncle to attend classes in NYC and abroad. When her son was diagnosed with severe asthma, she wanted to find drug-free solutions. She turned her culinary knowledge into research-driven healing—studying nutrition and enrolling at the Natural Gourmet Institute in New York.

> *I cooked my way through their 30-day meal plan. In
> 30 days, my son was off the meds. In six months, he
> was off everything—and he never went back.*

She prepared, froze, and shipped 180 meals that replicated the camp menu with healthy versions of the dishes served so he could attend camp safely. She continued to prepare special meals for years until he became stronger and built resilience. That kind of fierce persistence, research, and solution-generation became the foundation of her life and work.

At a dinner party, the school founder, Annemarie Colbin, tasted Minx's food and told her, "You really can cook." The next month, Minx started teaching.

> *I was terrified of standing up in front of people. Then*
> *I thought, 'Get over yourself. The world is in too much*
> *trouble for you to play small.' And that was that.*
> *Those words changed my perspective and my life!*

Minx learned not just to teach, but to speak—leading women's groups around that same kitchen table. Eventually, she contributed to the writing of *The Natural Gourmet*, nearly took over the school, and carried that momentum into her next chapter.

When Minx moved to Florida, she connected with women leaders and started creating transformational programs. A coach recognized what she was doing and told her, "What you're doing is called coaching. Go back and become a coach."

So, she did. Since 1999, Minx has coached women through life transitions, wellness challenges, and purpose-driven change. She calls herself a *health-wise and life-wise coach*, her practice rooted in lived wisdom and intentional action.

Minx has written more than 16 books and workbooks—and, as a creative and soul-searching practice, she writes a poem a day. You'll find one in each of her monthly newsletters. Much of this began during her initial breast cancer diagnosis, a time when she says:

> *I wasn't writing to publish. I was writing to stay sane*
> *and clear.*

She turned inward, journaling daily and asking two questions:

How do I want to show up NOW?

The answer that came to her was right there in the title of one of her more recent books: *Decades of Gratitude, Gusto, Grit and Grace.* Onward, with more of the same.

The other question was:

What do I want to return to?

The answer was cooking and exploring the enormous power and potential of food for healing.

Diagnosed with breast cancer, she leaned on her knowledge and lifestyle. She recognized that her cancer was stress-driven and made changes. She began journaling. She lowered her estrogen levels without medication, cooking her way through *Overcoming Estrogen Dominance* and other wellness-oriented books.

> *My oncologist said it wasn't possible. I said, 'Just watch me.' And he did.*

The diagnosis rekindled her purpose. She's teaching again—in North Carolina and locally—and speaking with holistic doctors about podcasting from a kitchen studio.

Four years later, Minx was diagnosed with Stage 4 metastatic cancer, and so, once again, she has turned her focus even more intently on healing at every level.

> *What I'm learning at this stage is that when I pray*
> *every morning, I pray for being able to live fully*
> *and accept all that is, even as I continue to focus on*
> *my healing. I don't want to just sit there dwelling*
> *on the cancer. I am doing what I need to do. I have*
> *a phenomenal ongoing team of support, but I don't*
> *want that to be all that my life is about at this time. So,*

*it's about moving forward in the middle of that. And
I am honestly grateful for all that I am learning and
exploring on this new healing journey.*

Minx leads small women's circles for what she calls Essential Conversations. She trained with The Center for Purposeful Living's Art of Convening and continues to create spaces for meaningful, magical dialogue.

*I still do that, and it's one of my favorite things in the
world.*

Ten years ago, she was asked to teach journaling at Florida Atlantic University. Since then, she's offered programs on self-discovery, resilience, and embodied presence. She also offers programs at retirement communities and assisted living facilities. Her most recent series drew from the previously mentioned book *Decades of Gratitude, Gusto, Grit, and Grace.*

*We all read tons of stuff. But knowing isn't doing.
What matters is integrating it—living it.*

Minx stands barefoot outside each morning to ground herself. She prays not for perfection, but for presence. Her guiding philosophy:

*I've been given this life—so I'll do something with
it. I want to live a meaningful, joyful life. One with
purpose.*

DEB ROTH
From Business to the Divine Feminine

I always wanted to be a teacher.
I played teacher as a kid, and I even minored
in education in college. But life had other plans.

D EB ROTH'S JOURNEY IS ANYTHING but linear, from her early aspirations of teaching to a corporate career in insurance and retirement planning, to becoming a coach, spiritual guide, and writer, and a facilitator who uses tools from astrology and Tarot to ancient rituals to help people navigate life's biggest transitions. Deb's path is a testament to embracing change and following one's passions.

At Mount Holyoke College, Deb majored in psychology and worked with children with learning disabilities, planning to pursue a master's degree in special education. But a sudden realization during her senior year changed everything:

I thought, 'I'm twenty-one and already in a rut!' So, I
moved to New York to see what else was out there.

Her corporate career began with Union Mutual Insurance as a service representative. Later, she moved to TIAA-CREF, where she thrived in a role that combined teaching and communication.

I traveled to Philadelphia and worked with

universities, giving presentations on pension plans—
there was the teacher in me.

When they were going to open a Philadelphia office, Deb didn't want to transfer.

> *By that time, I was married with two little boys and*
> *needed more balance. I ended up for two years as the*
> *VP of Administration for a small employee benefits*
> *consulting firm, working three and a half days a week,*
> *which was terrific. My affirmation that I would say*
> *every day on my way to work was, 'I have interesting,*
> *challenging part-time work that pays well and gives*
> *me more time with the boys.'*

It was during this transitional period that Deb began a deep investigation of the spiritual practices that would later define her life and career. Her husband, Peter, introduced her to astrology and channeling, sparking what Deb calls her "woo-woo journey."

She left the consulting firm in 1990 and helped her husband with his business for a couple of years.

> *It gave me flexibility, but it definitely didn't feed my*
> *soul in any way. And 1992 was one of those real*
> *pivotal years. I went with a friend to get a Tarot*
> *reading by a woman who was a therapist, Ellen*
> *Goldberg, and was blown away by what she told my*
> *friend. So, I went back and had my own session. And*
> *that blew me away.*

At the same time, she was shopping for a Unitarian Church in the City. She walked into 4th U and never left. It was there that she was introduced to the whole notion of the Divine Feminine.

That just cracked things open. It's like, Oh, my God! This is what has been missing in my own personal connection to the divine—this whole notion of the goddess.

From that moment, she started inhaling everything she could find about astrology, Tarot, women's spirituality, and the goddess. Somewhere along the way, Jung kept showing up. After about two years of this, she answered an ad for a counseling training program taught by therapists who were also astrologers. It was all the psychology stuff, but incorporated the archetypes of astrology.

That program became one of the key foundations of my master's program at Lesley College. I was fascinated by the archetypes of the four elements: fire, water, air, and earth. My master's thesis was titled, 'Weaving a Path of Wholeness Through Women's Ritual and the Four Elements.' It was, basically, like getting credit for doing what I loved the most.

"As I was getting ready to write the thesis at the end of '97, the co-director of my counseling program handed me an article in Money Magazine *about coaching. Because I kept saying to them, 'You know, I know I don't want to be a straight astrologer. I know I don't want to be a straight therapist. And what do I do?' And she handed it to me and said, "I think you're a coach." And she was right. It was like, oh, my God, you know? Like so many of us... That's what I am. I never knew what to call it.*

She began hosting women's circles, drawing on her love of ritual and connection.

> *The circles are a space for women to gather, heal, and grow. They're centered around New Moons, astrology, and seasonal spirituality. I've stopped downplaying the woo-woo aspect—it's what makes me unique.*

Over the years, Deb has expanded her work to include weddings, house blessings, baby namings, and Coming of Age ceremonies. One standout memory is a Coming of Age retreat she led for four girls and their mothers.

> *I had one wonderful little girl whose mom won my "Mystical, Magical Birthday Party" that I had donated to a school auction. For several years, from the time she was about 10 or 11, she would celebrate her birthday with her friends with my "Mystical, Magical Birthday Party." I taught them chants, and these girls had the most wonderful voices. I felt like I was surrounded by angels because, instinctually, they knew how to harmonize in these beautiful, clear, little girl voices. It was very, very special.*

Deb's coaching and ritual work have also intersected with her corporate experience.

> *After I became an interfaith minister, I started mentioning it during corporate workshops. Just that small disclosure opened up deeper conversations— people want to talk about what truly matters, not just their resumes.*

> *A great example of how this all came together*

*happened right after I finished my master's program.
I was hired as an adjunct consultant to do one-day
career transition workshops for an outplacement firm.
We'd start the day by introducing ourselves with an
'unusual thing about yourself.' Mine was that I was
an Interfaith Minister. That's all I said. And it was
so cool to watch how that simple thing opened up the
conversation in the room.*

*People started sharing how, while they still had
severance pay, they were going to go to an Ashram
in India. Another woman was going to open her own
astrology and metaphysical shop. It became about
the heart of career transition. And that was like, Oh,
my God. You know, you open the door just a little bit,
and people are so thirsty to have those kinds of heart-
based, authentic conversations about what's really
going on—not 'Just the facts, ma'am.'*

Looking forward, Deb is committed to embracing her unique blend of coaching, spirituality, and ritual.

*I've learned to stop apologizing for what I do. It's
not mainstream, but it's me, and it's what I'm here to
share.*

As our conversation ended, Deb reflected on the thread that ties her work together:

*It's all about service—helping people connect to
themselves, to each other, and to something greater.*

Through her story, Deb Roth reminds us that life's twists and turns are often the most illuminating—and that embracing your authentic self can lead to the most fulfilling work of all.

BEATTY COHAN
Staying in the Game of Life

When you're a competitive athlete, you never give up.
You figure out other ways to navigate,
change your strategy, change your mindset.

Beatty Cohan grew up in an Orthodox Jewish family in Winnipeg, the only child of a teacher mother and a writer father. Her father loved sports and nature, and her mother was the disciplinarian who kept a traditional home. Beatty, however, was not a good student. "I had no interest whatsoever in school, much to my mom's chagrin," she recalls. What her parents did recognize was the importance of keeping their daughter active.

She danced from age three, skated competitively throughout childhood, and learned tennis with her father.

> *Sports have really been, for me, a great*
> *antidepressant, anti-anxiety [tool], keeping you in*
> *shape. This is a lifelong lifestyle that I have, and I'm*
> *playing the best tennis of my life.*

Her competitive spirit showed itself early. At eleven, she insisted on entering the Manitoba Junior Tennis Championship despite never having played competitively.

*"They probably felt sorry for me because they
assumed I'd be out after the first round. But I won the
whole week. It taught me so much about winning and
losing."*

Sports gave her confidence, but so did an unexpected passion: advice. As a little girl, she devoured the *Dear Abby* and *Ann Landers* columns and stayed up late listening to a call-in counseling show.

*I remember thinking, wouldn't it be great if I had an
advice column or a counseling radio show?*

Years later, she would have both.
Despite her energy, Beatty was shy, she admits.

*I couldn't even say my name when I went to McGill for
graduate school.*

Realizing public speaking was essential to her career, she enrolled in a Dale Carnegie course at twenty-two. She said it changed her entire life.

With graduate training in marriage and family therapy and sexual dysfunction, she began as a school social worker in Montreal's inner-city schools. Soon she was promoted to director of the entire school social services program. Later, in Toronto, she worked for the Jewish Congress as a social planner and then became executive director of Jewish Family Services in Calgary, where she rebuilt the agency from the ground up.

Beatty eventually settled into private practice, but her career expanded in unexpected ways. She co-authored a book with her late husband, creating the *Never Make a Mistake in Love Again* program, which launched her national media career.

All of a sudden, we were everywhere—on television, in

the papers. It was very exciting.

She became a syndicated advice columnist, a radio host, and a frequent guest on national TV. For years, she ran *Ask Beatty* segments with ABC in Florida and now hosts a weekly show on the Progressive Radio Network. She co-authored a book with her husband, Elliot Cohan, titled *For Better, For Worse, Forever: Discover The Path To Lasting Love.*

Through it all, she has remained deeply committed to helping people navigate love and relationships.

> *I'm still on a mission to get my* Never Make a Mistake in Love Again *program out there. Despite all the self-help books, we are spiraling downward. But I know there are three things you have to do to never make a mistake in love again.*

Beatty's work has even intersected with politics. While living in Florida, Governor Jeb Bush appointed her to the state's marriage commission after seeing her on television. "For two years I was Commissioner Cohan," she laughs. It was eye-opening:

> *I was so naïve. I thought we would really get relationship education into the schools. The only people who cared were the teachers and guidance counselors. That was my first and last political experience.*

Her personal life has brought both loss and renewal. After nearly 30 years of marriage, her first husband died. Later, she reconnected with and married her current husband, Jim, a professor and activist.

> *He's opened my eyes to so many things I never*

*thought about before. Our wedding brought together
people like Reverend Barber and Cornel West—it was
extraordinary.*

Beatty describes herself as "aging backward." She exercises
daily, plays tennis with pros, and keeps a disciplined wellness rou-
tine.

*I feel ageless. I really do take care of myself, and I
don't have time for nonsense or toxicity. I'm very
careful about who I let into my personal life.*

Her philosophy is rooted in resilience, a lesson she credits to
her father and her years as an athlete:

*When you're a competitive athlete, you never give up.
You figure out other ways to navigate, change your
strategy, change your mindset. I've never had the
mindset of 'I'm going to give up.' It's just not there.*

She applies the same approach with her clients: acknowledg-
ing the past but focusing on the present.

*All we have is today. What can you do today to make
it a good day, even if yesterday was horrible?*

Beatty often shares the story of Charlotte, a client in her
mid-eighties who rediscovered romance after losing her husband of
sixty years. "She blossomed," Beatty recalls.

*She had affairs with much younger men—not
appropriate, but they didn't hurt her, and she felt
sexual until the day she died.*

Charlotte even asked Beatty to teach her intimacy skills.

*So we went into her kitchen with a banana. She died
at ninety, with a smile on her face, having lived with
passion until the end.*

For Beatty, Charlotte embodies the message she wants to pass on:

*We shouldn't allow age, wrinkles, or physical
problems to get in the way of doing what we love.
Passion, romance, vitality—they're possible at every
age.*

Beatty continues her private practice, her radio show, and her writing. She's experimenting with new platforms—her young social media consultant is teaching her TikTok—and pushing producers to bring her back on television.

Her purpose remains clear:

*It's all about helping people. Everything I do—my
practice, my columns, my shows—it's all under one
umbrella: helping people live the best possible lives
they can.*

And, she adds with conviction:

*It's about staying in the game of life. Never, ever
giving up.*

DONNA KARLIN
Coaching through the Shadows,
Leading in the Light

I connect with people where their deepest shadows lie.
That's where change begins.

Donna Karlin has never accepted limits. A pioneer in executive coaching and founder of *Shadow Coaching®*, she built an international reputation for helping leaders see themselves in action and grow from it. Her career has spanned orchestras, hospitals, boardrooms, and global conferences, but the common thread is resilience—and a refusal to stop learning.

As a child in Montreal, Donna dreamed of being a musician. At just sixteen, she auditioned for McGill.

> *I was accepted into the program only because it was*
> *a blind audition. This was the early seventies, and*
> *women didn't go into percussion.*

Despite being told she was too short to play, she wore four-inch heels to reach the top of the chimes. Soon she was playing with the Ottawa Symphony and the National Arts Centre Orchestra.

> *It was a lifelong dream, and I was able to realize that*
> *fantasy.*

Her performing career ended when she became a mother. Donna's son, Michael, was born with severe paralysis in one arm and shoulder. Doctors suggested radical amputations. She refused.

I called my brother, who was a surgeon, and told him: You need to do something.

Through persistence, she found a specialist, and Michael underwent a groundbreaking 15-hour procedure with 14 nerve grafts. His recovery required years of additional surgeries and intense therapy.

After he was showered, I had to blow-dry him with a hair blower because he couldn't be touched. The nerves would be just pulled out, just like if you pulled a root out from a plant if you mishandled it. Every day we went to the hospital. He had machines stimulating the nerves until they could grow into the muscles. That was my focus for the next two years.

Donna consistently helped Michael become independent.

Kids are smart. One day, he had to put a jacket on for us to go to the hospital, and I said to him, 'Okay, zip up your jacket.' Did you ever try doing a zipper up with one hand? And he was seven, something like that, and he was struggling. It was an hour, an hour and a half, and he was crying, and I was crying, and finally he said to me, 'Does it give you pleasure to watch me struggle?' Seven years old.

And I said to him, 'Would it give you pleasure to have your mother show up when you're in high school to

have to dress you because you can't do it yourself?'
And he just nodded, and he persevered until he figured
out how to do a zipper with one hand. Eventually,
he figured out how to tie a shoelace with one hand.
Try that one out. So, we put our heads together and
figured it out. If you knotted one end and put it at the
top and just laced one, you could do a slip knot and tie
your shoelace, because he didn't want to have Velcro
shoes like a baby when he was a teenager.

Her surgeon, watching Donna's ingenuity and dedication, urged her to help other patients. Donna had minored in anthropology and psychology along with her music degree and had to go back to school, train, and learn how to encourage without overwhelming.

I realized that if I were to work with all these patients,
I had to work with them on their level, which meant
continuously going back to school and studying and
speaking to world-class surgeons and figuring out
how far I could push the patients, because I couldn't
push them beyond what their capability was. I had
to help them enable themselves to do as much as they
could, just like I did with my son, because he watched
me and how I encouraged him to figure things out.

I started talking to the patients in the waiting room.
That's where the seed for Shadow Coaching® occurred
to me—people told me what they thought I wanted to
hear or what they wanted to feel. I realized if I could
observe them in context and see what the reality was,
I could really help.

Donna went on to talk about periodically asking herself what she's doing and what she wants to be doing, including who she wants to work with. She's been in this business for more than forty years and created the methodology that she's taught all over the world. In 2016, she received a call from her doctor telling her that she had breast cancer. She had a lumpectomy in early December and a second surgery just before Christmas. In mid-January, she went back to work while having radiation treatments.

Things settled down until 2018, when her home was destroyed by a tornado, displacing her and her husband. Her ex-husband decided to take her to court to challenge their divorce settlement—their thirteenth return to court.

> *His purpose was to bankrupt me through the legal system. He served me with papers demanding to know my prognosis, which was none of his business. That very day, I was re-diagnosed with cancer, which is none of his business.*

She could not have more radiation because of radiation saturation and radiation burns and was therefore scheduled for more surgery. Through it all, she kept working and innovating. She is a Founding Fellow of The Institute of Coaching. She served as President and Dean of the International Consortium for Coaching in Organizations, coaches TED Fellows and Senior Fellows, works with directors of the Sundance Institute, and her Fellowship programs work with corporate leaders, military, first responders, and innovators.

> *Then I asked myself, how do we bring what we do with the Fellows and at the Collaboratoriums, and that kind of thing, to corporate America, Canada, and*

*put together a program so that they have presence
on stage—and spread an idea to the higher-ups.
We're talking about the executives to potentially be
able to run with a program and innovation. So, in
other words, we're growing innovation from within a
company.*

She closed her school but realized that she didn't need to give up teaching. She's also becoming more discerning about who she chooses to coach. Most recently, she's been doing a lot of writing and has authored at least fifteen books, including *Inquiring Minds Want to Grow* and *Feedback Unfiltered.*

Even with decades of impact in executive development, Donna nurtures her own creativity. She's still working on ways to maintain balance and relax, including taking long weekends and cutting back on travel.

*That's what keeps me healthy. That's what keeps me
emotionally healthy. It's like when I apprenticed as a
pastry chef—that was just to keep me sane while I was
doing everything else. I quilt. I do all kinds of crafty
stuff. Now, I relax by painting porcelain. I lose track
of time with all the little tiny dots and designs.*

After more than forty years of reinvention, Donna continues to teach, coach, and write—while carefully choosing the clients who inspire her most.

From breaking barriers in a male-dominated orchestra to creating a world-recognized coaching methodology, Donna Karlin exemplifies persistence, creativity, and courage.

And for decades, she has been guiding leaders worldwide into the light.

There are days I wake up and think, 'What the hell happened?' But I have my health. I have my brain. And I have a voice. That's enough.

She keeps herself grounded with daily routines—meditation, journaling, and gratitude.

Every morning, I write down three things I'm grateful for. It changes your energy. You start to look for the good.

She also surrounds herself with positivity.

I don't watch the news at night. I don't dwell on negative people, and I say no a lot more than I used to.

Her advice to younger women? Don't wait.

So many women my age regret putting themselves last. Don't do that. Find your voice early and use it.

And to her peers?

It's not too late. Whether you're fifty, sixty, or seventy—your life isn't over. Reinvention is always possible.

DIANE DIRESTA
Owning the Room at Any Age

I'm in my seventies, and I'm still learning.
I think that's the secret—stay curious.

D IANE DIRESTA HAS SPENT HER life helping people find their voice—on stage, on camera, and in life. "My business is communication," she says, "and the biggest part of communication is confidence."

That confidence didn't always come naturally. Growing up in Brooklyn, Diane was a shy child who avoided the spotlight. "I was afraid to raise my hand in class," she recalls.

But when I had to speak, people listened. They told me
I had presence.

After earning degrees in Speech Pathology and Communication, Diane started her career in education and healthcare. But corporate life beckoned, and she eventually landed at Salomon Brothers, running their training and development center.

I loved teaching, but I knew I wanted to work for
myself. I walked away from a six-figure job to start
my own company.

She launched DiResta Communications in 1993, focusing on public speaking and executive presence. Her breakthrough moment came in 2002, when she self-published her book, *Knockout Presentations.*

> *That book changed everything. It opened doors. I became a media expert, and clients started coming to me.*

But success is about more than credentials.

> *You can have the best PowerPoint in the world, but if you don't believe in yourself, no one else will.*

She teaches her clients to speak with intention and clarity—and to own their space.

> *People think speaking is about words. It's not. It's about energy. How you show up.*

Her work has taken her around the world—from speaking engagements in the Caribbean to media training in Europe. But it's her recent pivot to video and digital platforms that excites her most.

> *COVID changed everything. Suddenly, everyone had to be on camera. And guess what? It exposed the cracks.*

Diane seizes the moment. She began teaching virtual presence, helping professionals adapt to Zoom, YouTube, and webinars.

> *You have to project warmth and credibility through a screen. It's a whole different skill set.*

She also rediscovered her love of video and got certified in

YouTube strategy.

*I'm in my seventies, and I'm still learning. I think
that's the secret—stay curious.*

Diane has always been ahead of her time. In the '90s, she taught a class on personal branding before the term went mainstream. Now everybody talks about branding; she was doing it before it was a buzzword.

Her own brand demonstrates the intersection of authority and approachability. On camera, she's polished but warm. Off camera, she's quick to laugh and deeply reflective.

She credits her family for her drive—and her courage.

*My parents believed in working hard, saving money,
and doing the right thing. That ethic is still with me.
My mother was fearless. She'd get on the subway
at 2 a.m. if she had to. My father was a tailor with
impeccable taste. I get my style from him.*

Style matters, Diane believes, especially as women age.

*I dress up for Zoom. I wear makeup. Not because I
have to—but because it makes me feel like myself.*

She's also blunt about the double standards women face.

*A man goes gray, and he's distinguished. A woman
goes gray, and she disappears. No, thank you.*

She points to a shift in the culture.

*Look at women over seventy now—Jane Fonda, Helen
Mirren. They're not hiding. They're showing up. That's
the model.*

For Diane, showing up means staying visible—on video, on LinkedIn, and in real life. She goes to events, speaks, and mentors. And she keeps learning.

She's thinking about a second book.

It's in there somewhere. Probably about aging boldly. With humor.

At seventy-five, Diane DiResta is still commanding rooms—virtual and otherwise.

Confidence is contagious. And guess what? It's never too late to catch it.

Diane refuses to disappear. When people ask when she's retiring, she says, "Why would I?" She loves what she does. She has control over her schedule; she chooses her clients. She sees this as the best chapter yet, still being clear about the challenges of aging.

Her advice to younger women? Don't wait.

So many women my age regret putting themselves last. Don't do that. Find your voice early and use it.

RITA BATTAT
Seeking Stories, Creating Connections

I really enjoy life. I enjoy doing things I like to do.
There's so much to do, and I think each person needs
to find their own thing. Have a good attitude, do what
you enjoy doing—take classes, do little things,
or just be lazy. That's okay too.

RITA HAS ALWAYS GRAVITATED TOWARD the stories that don't get told. Her most recent book began with a question few people ask: What happens to the other child in a family after a tragedy?

You hear about a death or an illness with a child in
the family, how it affects that child and the parents.
You don't always understand how the angst of the
parents trickles down to the other child, and then what
happens to that child.

That curiosity became a calling. As Rita began to seek out families for her book, "they came out of the woodwork. It was just amazing." The stories she uncovered revealed hidden dynamics, deep grief, and the lasting effects loss can have on a family system.

Rita's own story began in New York City, though her childhood was split between New York and Texas.

I missed New York and the New York way of life.

After college and years of travel, she returned to New York City for good. Her degree was in psychology, but Rita's path was anything but linear. She taught special education in Texas, but soon her interests took an unexpected turn into tea leaf reading—a practice she first did for entertainment, then as a business, and later as a form of intuitive coaching. She says of her eclectic career:

I'm a people person; I meet the most fabulous people— famous and not so famous and infamous. I loved it.

Rita's intuitive coaching was guided by her own natural instincts, something she traces back to her half-sister, who encouraged her to "think what you want" from a young age.

I didn't know it was different. Later on, I realized I used intuition to guide people—not just by the book.

Her travels were equally adventurous. As a teenager, Rita saved every penny she could—babysitting, birthday money—for the chance to see Europe. Her Bible was *Europe on $5 a Day*. She had a Eurail pass and would just take off for three months. She traveled with her best friend, sometimes splitting off to visit family in Israel or Iran, or to spend summers in Argentina with her older half-sister.

I was like Gidget—I had to get to the beach.

If she told her mother she wanted to go to school in Hawaii, her mother would pay; if it was just the beach, she wouldn't. So, she got to do that.

Rita's independent spirit set her apart, especially growing up as a Jewish girl from New York transplanted to Fort Worth, Texas, in the 1950s.

It was very prejudiced at that time. I was the darkest
person in my class.

She remembers the moment when a classmate told her,
"I can't talk to you anymore, you killed Jesus," and her mother's
response: "Tell her that she and her mother can go to hell." Rita
laughs, "It sort of went downhill from there."

Her personal history is deeply entwined with her work. Rita
lost a brother she never met—he died at fourteen, before she was
born—and her father died when she was still a toddler.

We had a very weird relationship, my mother and
me. I was always compared to my brother who was
always one step ahead.

It wasn't until years later, while talking with other mothers,
that Rita recognized subtle patterns in how grief and loss shape
family dynamics.

All of a sudden, it hit me—a little light bulb went off.
That's how this started.

The term "replacement child" is a psychological one, coined in
the 1960s to describe children born after the death of a sibling. "It's
a strange word, but it's an actual psychological term," Rita explains.
She is part of the Replacement Child Forum along with two other
women, all "replacement children" themselves, each of whom has
written a book on the subject.

It's really a condition of circumstance. It's what
happens emotionally. How is this child being treated?

Sometimes, she notes, it's not just the child born after; siblings who survive a loss or shoulder new responsibilities can be af-

fected, too.

Rita has never been content to follow a single path.

I sort of fall into stuff, and I'm just lucky that I have
this weird thing that I do.

Her intuitive readings, coaching, and connector's spirit have brought her into contact with countless people, from A-listers to ordinary individuals with extraordinary stories.

Each person has an incredible story. The other
thing that happens a lot is somebody will come that
you might not have connected with, and then you
understand where they're coming from—you feel it.
And then you really like them.

She's helped people find jobs, appeared at events, and even reunited families.

I found somebody's daughter whom they had adopted
out fifty-one years ago. I found her in three weeks, and
they got together—that was really wonderful.

Rita's gift is making connections, whether between people or within the hidden layers of their own lives.

Rita's marriage began with a twist of fate and a New Year's Eve party in New York. She had just moved back and was living with her cousin. Her future husband, then a sleep researcher at NYU, arrived at the same party by chance after an argument with his date.

We just talked the whole time. He came with me across
the park to walk my dog. My dog liked him. That was
good.

They married that July and have been together for forty-eight years.

She is now a grandmother, busy with friends and clients, and thinking about "another book," though she laughs that her husband would rather not hear her say it.

For Rita, achievement isn't always about big accomplishments. She feels that sometimes just reading a book is a really nice achievement during the day. She's learned to value being different and to appreciate the path she's carved for herself.

> *I've always been an odd duck. It wasn't fun when I*
> *was younger to be an odd duck, but then it was like,*
> *this is the way it's going to be.*

Rita looks back on her generation's activism with pride—pro-choice marches, antiwar protests, seeing Joan Baez in person.

> *We worked for what we got, but we always enjoyed*
> *it. There was always an enjoyment factor, and there*
> *were choices.*

She's proud of her independence and the satisfaction she found in making her own way.

> *There was a lot of satisfaction in making my own*
> *money. I felt good about that, and then I could do with*
> *it what I wanted to do.*

Her advice for women is simple but hard-won:

> *Find what you enjoy and do it. There's so much to do,*
> *and I think each person needs to find their own thing.*
> *Have a good attitude, do what you enjoy doing—take*
> *classes, do little things, or just be lazy. That's okay,*

too. Value being different. Life is meant to be lived, not measured by achievement alone.

Rita's greatest satisfaction comes from her connections—with her clients, with her family, and with the many stories woven through her own remarkable journey.

Each person has an incredible story. Famous or not famous, people have incredible stories.

Part 2
ARTISTS

THIS GROUP INCLUDES WOMEN IN diverse artistic endeavors. Common factors include exploration, continuous learning, and adaptation.

Christina Weppner has the most diverse path, yet it is clear how a core, continuously expanding skill set connects her choices. Her move from set designer to architect, combined with her childhood experiences, feels natural. Again, this is a good example of bricolage and openness to new things. She's been able to approach design from the theater-based perspective of best use of space.

Linda Ackerman's life continues to be full and rich, even as she's moved away from sculpture due to arthritis. Art continues to play a role in her life.

During our interview, she gave me a tour of creations made from objects collected in her travels. She has a true artistic sensibility as well as a long history of service to others.

Harriet Forman Barrett has always been an artist. I'm one of her many loyal fans and adore each of my Harriet jewelry pieces. She's overcome adversity, including bias and illnesses, and has continuously adapted. This includes dealing with ever-rising gold prices, causing her to consider more work in silver. Her paintings and sculptures also continue to evolve as she experiments with new materials.

Gabrielle Carlson is passionate about dressing women to embrace who they are, as they are.

Lynne Levin has been an artist since childhood and has created a successful and enjoyable career as a fashion illustrator and professor. We met through our mutual friend, Phylis Haynes, and discovered that her dear friend, who had recommended her for the faculty positions, is a distant cousin of mine.

CHRISTINA WEPPNER
Bringing Theatrical Design to Architecture

The visual understanding of beauty is so important to me.

CHRISTINA LEARNED SELF-RELIANCE AT AN early age. This involved learning a wide range of skills: hammering, nailing, wiring, painting walls, leveling shelves, installing standards—all the kinds of stuff that you do around the house. The first time she ever had to install a set of bookshelves, she was about nine. Her parents felt art was important, so she started taking painting classes after school when she was about ten and life drawing classes at a local college the summer she turned thirteen.

When she was ready to go to college, she thought of being an architect because she loved spending time with her father, who was a noted architect, but her mother thought that it was much too hard a job for a woman. Then, she decided that what she wanted to do was throw wonderful parties in foreign countries for interesting people. She was going to study European History and French, and work for the diplomatic service in a foreign country, and give wonderful parties for people. However, she discovered that they really wanted people who knew a lot about economics rather than culture.

Then she thought about being a cultural attaché.

Christina went to Connecticut College, took European History and French, and was enjoying that. Then, a dorm friend's grandmother got sick, and she had to leave the winter production of a show with the drama club where she was the wardrobe mistress. She asked Christina to fill in for her and gave her a bunch of safety pins and said, "If anything happens, just pin them together, and they'll go back on stage."

Nothing went wrong. When the friend returned, she invited Christina to help her finish painting the set of another show she was involved with in the drama club.

The next fall, a new faculty advisor for the drama club said he'd heard Christina was handy and asked if she wanted to design the set for the first show, *Hansel and Gretel*. He showed her a picture of two exterior walls of a little cottage that was very cartoony against a kind of backdrop that had a few woodsy trees and bushes.

And I said, 'I think I can do that.' And, by golly, I have no memory of how it happened. But obviously something happened, and there was a set.

Then, the next show, they asked if she wanted to do the costumes. It was all togas. There were about fifty costumes, a lot of people, and Christina ended up staying up five nights in a row on NoDoz to make it all happen.

Shortly after, the faculty advisor took her out for coffee at the student union and said, "You are wasted at this school. I think you really have what it takes to design for the theater, and you've got the persistence. You've got the drive. You've got the vision. And I think you've got to leave here and go study to do this professionally. I have a great place for you to go. I know people who teach at the school, and I will write you such a great letter of recommendation that they would be foolish not to take you."

She talked to her parents about it, and they thought that it was a good idea. She transferred to the NYU School of the Arts and became a member of the third graduating class.

> *All the people teaching were working professionals*
> *— very good professionals. It was a wonderful,*
> *wonderful time: an amazing, free-flowing time. We*
> *had an extraordinary class, most of whom I'm still in*
> *touch with to this day.*

She worked in the theater for fifteen to sixteen years: Broadway, Off Broadway, Off Off Broadway, way Off Broadway. She describes it as:

> *Here, you've got $35 you can spend on the set. Make*
> *the set, use our stock, build it yourself, and I think we*
> *have a carpenter for a day or two to help you out.*
> *Or it was somebody's brother, a cousin, a boyfriend,*
> *whoever would show up with a hammer and help. It*
> *was just an amazing time, and I really loved it.*

In the early '80s, a show from the WPA Theater moved to Broadway, and she was the designer who took over. She kept getting bigger shows, including designing several Shakespeare plays at the Public Theater for Estelle Parsons, as well as designing shows at La Mama and Playwrights Horizons. Her Off-Broadway productions had casts that included Helen Gallagher, Swoozy Kurtz, Mary Beth Hurt, Polly Draper, Tammy Grimes, Dan Florek, and James Rebhorn.

She had been working in different theaters, and when a director loved your work, they'd call you the next time they had a show. That's how it worked: you create little teams of people. You'd be the set designer. Someone else would be the costume designer. Someone else would be the lighting designer. And then you'd work together on a production — that's how it works.

She had several teams of people she was working with. She was their preferred designer and did some wonderful shows. Eventually, after doing three to four of those blockbusters back-to-back, she was exhausted. So, since she had passed the Set and Costume Design exams in her final semester at NYU and was a member of Local 829, the Union of Theatrical Designers, she had an idea. She dusted off her scenic brushes and passed the Scene Painting exam. Now she could put her name on The List and get calls for freelance work for Broadway, TV, and films— just show up, paint miles of marble. No pressure!

> *I was so exhausted from always designing, but I still*
> *needed to work. But I just wasn't willing to take on*
> *any substantial responsibility.*

There was a list for these openings. When people needed someone, they would call in and say, "Who's on The List?" Her income tripled instantly, and she enjoyed the variety of assignments. She turned down work as a designer for a couple of years. At a certain point, it became clear to her that scene painting wasn't as satisfying as designing.

When Christina started calling around, she found that things had changed. Her Special People had moved to the West Coast or switched to academia. Theatrical production managers had new set designers.

She spent two years doing industrials—corporate events in hotel ballrooms, with a theme related to the product that they're promoting and bringing to market. It could be an award ceremony, all glamour and Hollywood. She was on the Board of Women in Theater NY and designed their one-act play festival for several years. She enjoyed working with other women in theater but felt her career wasn't moving forward.

Unhappy with her career situation and losing a relationship she was in because she didn't want to get married, she went into therapy. After reevaluating her life, she decided that her skills were well-suited to architecture, so she took a course at Pratt to study Historic Preservation. It turned out to be more scientific and analytic than she expected. She did like the school, though, and enrolled in their Architecture Program.

She went on to an internship at Gwathmey Siegel. It was very important for her in terms of her overall development, and she had a wonderful time.

After that, she became business partners with an old friend—he had been her mentor for the architecture exams—and they worked together for the next fourteen years. They remain friends.

> *I've never found anybody as close and trustworthy as*
> *I did in that relationship with a business partner. I've*
> *worked with various other people, but I've never had*
> *the same sense of utter reliability that I had with him.*

John is the man who wanted to marry Christina in the early '80s. They were both in the theater, and he still is. He was president of his own production company, and he and his wife did a lot of work for various corporations. Around 2009, he sent her a request to connect on LinkedIn because he'd seen an article in the *New York Times* about a book that E. L. Doctorow had written about the Collyer brothers. He was still married, so they became just Facebook friends, and he would send her a joke every month or two. It was through Facebook that she learned his wife died.

*I sent my sympathy, and about ten months later, I
invited him to come to a family wedding. By the time
we met up again six weeks later, after multiple weekly
phone calls, we knew each other significantly better
than we had. He ended up coming to New York for
Thanksgiving, and when he left after about ten days, I
knew I wanted him to always be there.*

Christina loves what she's doing now.

*I think I learned everything about design while I was
designing for the theater, because when you design
a play, you read the script. That is the world of the
piece. Then it's informed by other information, but
it's basically the world. And so, as a set designer, I
always wanted to have anything that the characters
that I saw in the script might conceivably want to do
as part of their personality, to further the story, or just
express themselves, or whatever, ought to be able to
happen.*

As an architect, Christina translates that into people's lives.
She gets a sense of who they are and what all the possible uses of a
space might be.

*What is it that they're going to do that can be done?
How can we make it possible? How can we make it as
close to possible as possible?*

She accepts that New York apartments tend to be on the small
side and works to make them flexible. She had been very excited
about designing a preschool when COVID hit.

I have the idea of making a space that would excite

*and inspire. The visual understanding of beauty is so
important to me. I can't tell you how much I long to
do that project. I love it. And there it was—working
with families in that way to make something that
awakens curiosity and the love of beauty in a kid and
is functional for the teachers.*

LINDA ACKERMAN
A Life Shaped By Art, Community, and Strong Family Bonds

Find your truth and tell it, and anybody who doesn't want to hear it doesn't belong in your life. That's it. Period.

Linda was born in 1938 and grew up on Pelham Parkway in the Bronx, surrounded by cultural sites including Orchard Beach, the Bronx Zoo, and the Botanical Gardens. When her father contracted tuberculosis, the family moved to Liberty, New York—a Borscht Belt community, a popular Jewish vacation destination, and a growing Jewish community.

> *When I talk about Liberty to Jewish people my age, they think, oh, it's so Jewish up there! Everybody has a Catskill Mountain story. They all met their spouses and so on. And there are wonderful Catskill memories and stories. I worked in the summertime because it provided the income, the livelihood, for us all for the entire year. So, it was not a vacation land for us— quite the opposite.*

Linda's parents modeled community leadership and discretion.

*My mother had this unofficial psychiatric practice.
She gave loving guidance to so many people...after she
passed, we got letters of gratitude that made us weep.*

Her father was less sociable but had a more global intelligence
about human nature.

*He was a reader, a Jewish gym teacher, and later
taught everything, including to disabled and retarded
young people.*

Linda describes her upbringing as a blend of practicality and
optimism:

*We are just plain people who knew how to put it
together, who knew how to cooperate with one
another. Though they had many differences, they
respected and loved one another, and they had self-
respect, which is the root of it all.*

She attended Barnard on a scholarship, an opportunity she
credits to her small-town background:

*Had I stayed in the Bronx, I never would have gone to
Barnard. Coming out of Liberty, New York, I looked
like a star. I was second in my class out of sixty-seven
students. I had a really weak education compared
with the girls from Brooklyn—God damn it, they
were amazing—but I found out that in the long run
it doesn't matter all that much. If you have the right
genes and finally have the opportunity, you begin to
flower.*

Linda met her husband, Bill, at Barnard.

*We were engaged in six weeks from the day we met,
because it was love at first sight. Bingo!*

They married after college, and Linda quickly became immersed in family life.

*I was mothering right off the bat and didn't have a
chance to find out more about myself. Many of my
friends went on to careers, but only part-time, because
once they started their families, they were at home.*

Despite her creative inclinations, Linda put aside her interest
in art until later in life.

*I probably sublimated an interest in expressing myself
artistically. That's a much later chapter.*

She eventually discovered sculpture almost by accident:

*I misread the adult education catalog. I thought I was
going to learn how to throw pots. It was such an eye-
opener. I didn't know I had any talent—not that I had
no talent—just that nobody told me. We didn't live in
an environment where that was valued.*

Linda became a figurative sculptor, capturing friends and
family in clay—often working from visual memory. Her father's re-
action to his own portrait was unforgettable:

*He looked at me—he was just amazed, because he saw
himself, and he said, 'Oh, my God! When did you get
to be so talented?' And I said, 'I must have come that
way.'*

Community involvement remained central.

I was joining every PTA and committee I could to enrich and enhance educational experiences for my children—in other words, my family and myself as well. Bill and I created a new educational track in our religious school in our temple—experiential education, requiring parental and familial involvement—that's wonderful!

She also worked in Jewish cultural arts, despite not being formally trained.

I know that many good seeds fell in the communities because of my work. But I'm the one who was the real beneficiary here, let me tell you, and my family as well.

Her creative journey continued into her sixties and seventies, though arthritis has limited her sculpting.

Now I make these little scenes all over my house. Most of my living room is souvenirs from various trips, and what's not a souvenir is pictures—which are souvenirs—people, places, or things.

Linda's home reflects her tactile and visual sensibility.

When I walk into the contemporary home that's gray and beige and white, and there are no tchotchkes around, I don't know anything about the people who live there except that they seem really blank and bland to me. Oh, what about these homes that don't have books in them? That's a person's life that you're seeing in their bookcases.

Asked what brings her the greatest joy, Linda's answer is simple:

My children and grandchildren. My children are all really, really in the last few years finding their groove and their voices...It's interesting to see how Rebecca has gone from being a meticulous linear lawyer to being Rebecca—a teacher, writer, editor, storyteller.

Her advice for other women:

Find your truth and tell it, and anybody who doesn't want to hear it doesn't belong in your life. That's it. Period.

Linda concludes with gratitude for her family and her life's journey:

I'm a really happy girl. I am grateful. I pay homage every day to my amazing parents. Once the lessons are learned, they're learned.

HARRIET FORMAN BARRETT
Fierce, Fearless, and Forever Creating

I always was an artist. That was my escape. That was my way of having space for myself in a family that was a bit dysfunctional.

EARLY ON, SHE WAS PRAISED for her creativity—as long as it didn't interfere with the rigid expectations of her conservative Jewish upbringing. Her father wanted her to become a secretary and get married.

> *I was the oldest girl. I had to blaze a trail for my two*
> *younger sisters. I got the brunt of it, and then they*
> *could secretly do whatever they chose.*

Harriet attended the High School of Music and Art. She left home to attend Pratt Institute, waitressing to support herself, and focused intensely on her art. Along the way, she lost some girl-friends because someone would say, "Oh, she likes her art," and the girls didn't like hearing that. It was as if it empowered them by saying that, and a lot of times she stayed home from certain classes.

> *I couldn't achieve what I wanted, but I knew my gifts*
> *were in my body. If something didn't fit me, it felt like I*
> *was being suffocated to death.*

Her art was a lifeline. It was her survival, her meditation. Over time, she expanded from painting to sculpture and jewelry.

Though fiercely committed to women's rights, she often found herself dismissed, even in her own booth when she was exhibiting her sculptures at an art exhibit.

Women would come up and ask the man next to me
about my sculptures. They treated me like I was just
the good wife.

Once, when she became successful enough to be in books and magazines, a rumor started that she got her prestigious booth space by sleeping with the photographer.

I got him the job! And suddenly, none of my work
mattered.

She fought for women's rights but didn't fight for herself when this happened; instead, she shriveled and, in effect, became invisible.

Now, looking back, it enrages me that I lost that
momentum. But everything has its purpose.

That pain enriched her work, as dealing with it furthered the sense of empowerment that is imbued in her art. Her work is unmistakably feminine and full of life. Her message has always been *Life is One.*

It's about joy, about remembering who we are.
Whether it's the figure, the movement, or how a piece
flows on your body, it's about empowerment.

She speaks of a magical moment at a show at Mohonk when

women gathered at her booth, laughing, talking, buying art, and supporting one another. One woman from Texas, who helps survivors of abuse, bought a ring for another woman who was grieving her husband. "She said, 'He always bought me jewelry.'"

We all hugged and cried. That whole weekend was like
that. That's what my work is about.

Over the years, she's had to navigate jealousy, power plays, and male dominance in the art world.

Harriet said that when it became lucrative, the men jumped in and got all the recognition. They even used her motifs. She noted that no one honors the past in this field. Harriet doesn't hold back. She's called out men who tried to take credit or space from women.

I've learned to use their guilt to keep them in check, but
I do it with humor—I tickle people into awareness.

Health challenges didn't stop her. She battled Lyme disease that spread to her brain—and kept working through it.

I used a wheelchair in my house just to keep creating.
I'd do a show, then go right to bed. That was my
lifeline.

Later, she fought cancer, discovered almost accidentally during a Lyme flare. She chose not to have reconstructive surgery and endured treatment her own way.

Every time I had chemo, I'd sit by the fire and rest.
Somehow, I always made it to the next show.

She also took on the care of her traumatized grandchildren at an age when most people are retiring.

They weren't used to being parented. They thought structure was abuse. I wasn't their grandmother anymore—I was the authority figure they didn't want.

The experience was exhausting but transformative.

Now they're adults, and we get to know each other as people. It was worth it.

Her art continues to evolve. Jewelry had been her primary focus for several years, although she continued to paint and sculpt. Those lucky enough to own her jewelry instantly recognize each other, and admire each other's pieces.

I'm painting more, sculpting, and showing in galleries again. COVID gave me time to go deep. Some pieces are about grief, others about resilience. My work has always been spiritual—you either feel it, or you walk right by.

Harriet invokes the power of collective spirituality, the feminine, the empowerment of being, and the careful balance within that. Her artwork is in private collections around the world. Recent exhibitions include Lace Mill Gallery '24-'25, One Woman Show at Wired Gallery, '24, Bank Art Gallery '25, and Arbor Gallery '25. She has a one-woman show opening un Woodstock in March, 2026.

She still does shows, with help from young assistants who see firsthand what it takes to live a creative life.

I can't lift what I used to or drive at night, but I adapt. I'm not stopping. People ask when I'll retire, and I tell them, 'When I'm dead.'

Harriet encourages older women to stay vital.

We're not done until we're done. You have to find your
vitality and go for it, even if it's scary. Tiptoe out.
Try something new. You don't know your gift until you
try it.

She laughs, remembering a fellow jeweler who called her "a tribute to all of us" for her perseverance.

I never thought about it that way. I just do my thing.
But I'll keep doing it until the end. This is my life, and I
love it.

GABRIELLE CARLSON
Dressing Women to Feel Beautiful

I dress women to be their best selves; to feel beautiful and communicate a sense of who they are.

GABRIELLE WAS BORN IN SOUTH Africa. Her parents were both political activists, working with Nelson Mandela, and it became time for them to move to the United States in 1971 after bombs were sent to their family home. They settled on Long Island, and she and her three siblings were heading for their first day of school:

> *We were getting ready to go to school—having no idea of how to dress. And I'm the eldest of four kids; we'd just arrived. I was wondering what best to wear on the first day of school in a new country, when I knew that even though we're speaking English, we're not going to understand a lot of what's going on. My mom was also clueless about what to wear for our showing up at school: We'd always worn uniforms. My mom thought that the best thing to do was to be respectful. Thinking about it, I'm reliving how mortified I was. My hair was very long, in a ponytail. I was wearing my best dress, lace tights, and black patent shoes—*

dressed in my best clothes. Wrong!!!

Shortly after arriving at school, Gab found a phone and asked her mother to come and get them immediately. It was the height of the Vietnam War, and kids in this liberal community were all wearing torn jeans, beads, long hair, t-shirts — and possibly no shoes.

Our clothing said, 'We do not belong.' In hindsight,
there are some funny aspects to it, but at the moment
when you're ready to go through the floor, it was
mortifying.

She remembers going to buy the same clothes that some of the girls wore. Yet even that didn't feel right.

I'm not that body. It's not how I dress. Outside of
uniforms, I've always kind of done my own thing,
without questioning it.

People she dresses, too, know what they like, even if they can't define it. And they know, as soon as they put something on, if it isn't them.

If I'm not comfortable in what I'm wearing, it's hard
for me to get on with whatever is needing to be done. I
have to change first. Then I'm settled and can take on
anything.

Gabrielle dressed women long before she started to design. After graduating from the New School, she began working at Bergdorf's, where, after a short while, she was recruited by Barney's New York to open their first women's store on 17th Street, overseeing the 'New Designers' floor. She was initially excited, but it became 'a bit of a travesty' because the General Manager, the woman who oversaw buying clothes for the store, was a size four-six and wore dressy clothing. There was nothing for older women, and very few pieces for women larger than a size six or eight. The only size ten on her entire floor was a Victor Edelstein dress. He's a British designer who dresses royalty and celebrities…and it was a $10,000 dress.

My passion is dressing women: I love fabric and drape, I am drawn to color—only, at this point, I don't know how to pattern, cut, or sew. One of my key strengths is that I am able to attract a team of people. I was lucky enough to find patternmakers, a cutter, and sewers, most of whom are with me to this day.

From this beginning, Gabrielle started designing and had a series of stores and salons across Manhattan, from the Village to the Upper East Side. Wherever she is, Gabrielle's salon has always been a magical place, full of color, beautiful garments, and a community of customers who have become lifelong friends. Women who are dressed by Gabrielle—her tribe—recognize each other on the street and tell stories of their favorite Gabrielle outfits or experiences in the salon. She has hosted trunk shows, book signings, and the occasional birthday party. Often, members of Gab's tribe would offer opinions to others in the salon or pitch in and help. There is always an atmosphere of joy in her presence.

I love dressing women, many of whom doubt themselves—feeling unsure of their still being attractive post their youth. Women who are so alive, have experienced much, have impacted the world they live and work in, yet feel their best lives are behind them. They are very much alive, many of them just coming into their own—or so it seems to me!

*It's wonderful to be in a position where you can
be part of someone finding themselves attractive,
enjoying how they look, and, more than anything,
feeling like it's far from over. They are enjoying
themselves. And what's particularly fun is dressing
women who are mothers in a bridal group. I enjoy
doing this — I create specifically for the women I
dress.*

With retail rents skyrocketing in New York City, Gabrielle chose to close her most recent salon on Lexington Avenue and 74th Street a year ago. She was recruited by Bloomingdale's flagship NYC store, where she continues to do what she loves to do—dress women to be their best selves. At the same time, she continues to create clothes for her faithful customers, whom she continues to dress. Many of her clients visit her at Bloomingdale's—experiencing her styling skills wherever she may be! Gabrielle will continue dressing the women who love wearing her clothes—and their friends and family, whom they bring to her.

In October 2025, Gabrielle had a trunk show in the Guerlain Spa at the newly renovated Waldorf Astoria. Friends and clients filled the beautiful space, full of beautiful Gabrielle Carlson originals as well as accessories from Kate Beck and jewelry from Laura Kass. As we chatted over champagne and small snacks, we connected with friends and offered advice on choices. Gabrielle will continue to present her pieces and establish community with her clients for many years to come.

Whatever the future offers Gabrielle, you can be sure that her magic will continue.

LYNNE LEVIN

Artist, Fashion Illustrator, Professor

What I plan to do is to keep on keeping on.

LYNNE WAS AN ARTIST FROM childhood. It was always her strong suit. She went to the University of Maryland in College Park, which she says was a great place.

> *I started my career having won a contest, a national contest for* Mademoiselle *Magazine. And it was just when I had just finished my last day of college, I was on a train to New York, and that was the beginning of my career. And I've been working in the fashion industry ever since as an illustrator.*

> *My goal was always to be a fashion illustrator, and very soon I began working for Macy's, which was a full-time gig where I was there every day, and we drew from the model, and that's how it began. So, I've been illustrating for retail and also for the ad agencies for a long, long time.*

And then she decided to become a regular artist, and learned how to paint and draw from life.

I was always taking courses while I was working. And then I had a family, so that came in between. But the point is that I developed— I studied and practiced. I drew and painted my whole life, basically, at the Society of Illustrators and the Art Students League. I had wonderful teachers at the Art Students League, specifically, where I learned how to paint. And I've been painting ever since.

And now I teach because of your cousin, Pat Porter, whom I met at a workshop many, many years ago. When she decided to retire, she said, 'Do you want to teach my course? I'm going to retire.'

And I said, 'Well, no, because I'm too busy working.' And she said, 'Well, come on, just show them your portfolio.' And so I went. I got the job, and I've been teaching there ever since, which is to say thirty years—at Parsons, at the New School.

Linda teaches fashion illustration, and the course is called Design Sketching.

It's really wonderful for me, and the students seem to like it, and they're from all over the world. It is nice. Because of my great love of teaching, as well as art, I became very familiar with my students, like our friend Gab Carlson, who was a student of mine at Parsons. That's how we met. The rest is history. We became friends, and I'm very much one of her circle of people who admire her fashion—very much so, and I'm sporting it today.

Teaching is a marvelous, marvelous thing, and now we teach on Zoom, where I have a class of sixteen. I have two courses per semester, and I've been doing that. So that's a side gig, and it's been wonderful.

Life and fashion have been wonderful, and I've been able to do it as a mother. That was part of why I wanted to be an artist; you could kind of make your own hours.

Lynne's career has given her ample time with her family while she was raising her children.

It did, it did, and it still does. So, I mean, they're all grown now. I have two wonderful boys—men. But the life of an illustrator is a wonderful thing. You get to really meet some incredible people, and it's been a joy for me to have done that.

It's fun. As an illustrator, I used to work for a lot of big agencies as a freelancer, which is to say you come in, not on staff. But I've met some incredible illustrators that way. They gave me great inspiration—some of my compatriots, my friend Edmund Ng, who is a brilliant illustrator, and people whom I met along the road. It's been a world of wonderful people that I've been exposed to. I've been lucky enough to work with.

Being a woman has never been a hindrance to me. As a matter of fact, I just want to mention that I've never been asked for my degree. Nobody's ever asked me for my credentials, my college degree, or anything like that. And, as a woman, I've always felt completely equal and not in any way discriminated against, so that's been a wonderful part of it.

She doesn't know if she's going to continue teaching.

I love the teaching, and I don't know whether I'll continue teaching, but I hope to. I don't see any reason why I wouldn't, unless there's no enrollment because of the political climate, which we won't talk about, but just to say, Parsons gets students from all over the world, as you know. And so it's been a big issue whether or not the courses will be able to be filled that way. But I teach on Zoom, so I don't know whether that would really even be a problem for me. But we'll see whether they continue the structures the way they are.

It's all good as far as that's concerned, and I plan to keep making art, doing my art, and doing my painting. And people could certainly look at my website, which is Lynnlevin.com.

And it's been a wonderful journey all these years. Being in New York and being exposed to everything that we have here, the museums and the galleries, is a wonderful life.

So, what I plan to do is to keep on keeping on. There it is. I mean, you've got the short version of my story, and I'm happy to share it with you.

Part 3
COMMUNITY CREATORS

THESE WOMEN ARE MULTI-TALENTED. WHAT stands out for each of them is that, in addition to busy careers, they have consistently created and expanded communities.

Cheryl Benton created a lifestyle newsletter that grew into a nationwide community for women over forty. The Three Tomatoes now hosts annual wellness summits, and she has expanded her brand into book publishing—The Three Tomatoes Publishing.

Randie Levine-Miller has always been ready to extend a helping hand. In her public relations career, she mentored several newcomers. At the Friars, she hosted lunches, bringing together theater professionals. After leaving the Friars, she kept the tradition alive by creating Randie's Roundtable.

Francene Katzen began creating community as she worked to help her daughter move beyond addiction. Today, she is an advocate for parents of children with addictions, hosts a book group, and, as often as possible, hosts Three Tomatoes' authors.

Holli Gresh spent many years working to elect pro-choice women. She sits on the boards of NYU Steinhardt's Dean's Council, the Tri-State Maxed Out Women PAC, and *We Care*, which supports survivors of domestic abuse.

Deborah Konigsberger's background in modeling and fashion

led her to open the boutique that led to the creation of Hearts of Gold to help women and children in shelters. At the time of this writing, her organization has helped over 40,000 women.

CHERYL BENTON
Growing The Three Tomatoes

Put yourself out there. Engage with other people. Join a group, volunteer, help someone—it gets you out of your own head.

WHEN CHERYL BENTON LAUNCHED *The Three Tomatoes* in 2006, it was more of a passion project than a business plan. Her husband challenged her to treat The Three Tomatoes like one of her marketing clients. She realized he was right. Cheryl folded her consulting business and focused on seeing how far she could take this online lifestyle resource for women over forty.

> *I owned an ad agency on Long Island for ten years. We had a lot of high-tech companies as clients. And then, very close to the ten-year mark, my agency got acquired by a big ad agency in New York City. Years before I started my ad agency, I was marketing director for a global tech company, where I managed the advertising budget and our ad agency. But when I wanted to move to the ad agency side, the ad agencies did not want to hire me because I didn't have "ad agency experience" unless I went through one of their training programs, which was usually for recent*

college grads. I said, no thanks, and started my own agency. Well, the agency that acquired me was one of those that didn't want to hire me. I always thought, you know, revenge is sweet.

So, I joined them. That's how I got into the advertising agency world. I really loved that side of the business, and that was where I spent the next ten years of my career before leaving advertising to start my own marketing consulting firm and then starting The Three Tomatoes.

When I stepped out of that world and into the world of The Three Tomatoes, *it just opened up these amazing opportunities and chances to meet so many people whom I just would never have met had I stayed in that advertising circle.*

For example, I was very involved for several years with UN Women. It was really through a Three Tomatoes *subscriber who reached out to me and said, "I love what you're doing and how you're focusing on women giving back and women supporting organizations that help women. I'd like to tell you about this group." I joined the board and went on to become president of the NYC Chapter of UN Women, supporting women and girls around the globe.*

Cheryl talked about those first years of *The Three Tomatoes* when unexpected champions showed up, offering both encourage-ment and contributions that helped the newsletter blossom.

When I first launched the newsletters, I hid behind
The Three Tomatoes name. I wasn't sure yet that
what I was sending out truly mattered to women,
and honestly, I was afraid of criticism. Then, at our
one-year mark, everything changed. I received an
unexpected email from Valerie Smaldone—a five-time
Billboard Magazine Award winner and the longtime
midday host of 106.7 Lite FM. She told me she loved
the newsletters, knew our anniversary was coming
up, and wanted to help plan an event so people could
meet the "tomato" behind The Three Tomatoes.

I was stunned. My first thought was, "Why would
anyone want to meet me?" But Valerie insisted,
planned a fabulous event, and over 100 women
showed up. She soon began contributing theater
reviews, and that was the start of a wonderful
friendship. We've done several events together, and
she remains one of our biggest champions."

And Valerie wasn't the only early "celebrity" supporter.

One night at a dinner hosted by an Italian tourism
group, I heard a familiar voice—Arthur Schwartz,
"The Food Maven," restaurant critic for the Daily
News *and a regular on Joan Hamburg's radio show.*
To my delight, he sat next to me. He had just lost both
his newspaper and radio positions, so I invited him to
contribute to The Three Tomatoes. *His food and recipe*
column became a beloved feature for years.

A few days later, he called to say his good friend

Gael Greene was also interested in contributing. Gael Greene! The legendary, razor-witted restaurant critic whose reviews were known nationwide. She, too, had recently lost her column at New York Magazine. *Of course, I said yes, and her reviews appeared on our site for many years until her passing."*

Then came another surprise—an email from a newsletter subscriber named Liz Smith. Yes, *that* Liz Smith, the iconic gossip columnist.

"Her note said, "Read my column in today's New York Post.*" There it was: 'According to* The Three Tomatoes, *Helen Mirren was spotted on the subway on her way to an awards ceremony when she couldn't get a cab.'*

Naturally, I reached out, and for many years, we ran her column on our site until her death. I still treasure the many encouraging notes she sent me.

Her first major expansion came after connecting with Los Angeles actress Debbie Zipp. Debbie had been producing humorous videos about women and aging with three fellow actresses.

We just really connected, even before we met in person.

Together, they launched *Tomatoes in the Trenches,* a coast-to-coast talk radio show featuring Cheryl and her daughter Roni on the East Coast, and Debbie with two actress friends on the West Coast. Eventually, Debbie began publishing the Los Angeles edition of *The Three Tomatoes* newsletter.

*From the start, even though we were New York–
focused, our second-largest audience was always L.A.
There was just always a connection there.*

Partnerships followed. In New York, Cheryl began co-hosting an annual *Renewal Summit* with Anne Akers and launched *Tomatoes Got Talent* with Randie Levine-Miller. These events built visibility, and the platform grew beyond a newsletter to a true lifestyle resource.

Originally, *The Three Tomatoes* featured events and products for women of a certain age, but as more contributors came aboard, its content deepened. Today, it covers health and wellness, fitness, style, and travel—often with credentialed experts whose own networks help amplify its reach. In addition to New York and Los Angeles editions, Cheryl has added San Francisco and Miami newsletters and dreams of a London edition someday.

Writing a book had been on Cheryl's mind for years. At first, she envisioned a nonfiction guide for midlife and beyond, drawing on wisdom she'd gathered through *The Three Tomatoes*, but the project stalled.

I couldn't get excited about it—it felt forced.

Then one day, on a train from Manhattan to Long Island, the first sentence of a novel popped into her head.

*As soon as I flipped the switch to fiction, I knew I had
it. I could get the message across in a much more
engaging, entertaining way.*

That summer, in about three months, she wrote *Can You See Us Now?*—the story of three women proving that life after fifty is far from over.

Publishing industry veterans advised her to skip the traditional route, saying, "You have a built-in platform. Publish it yourself." She did—and the novel found its audience. That success led to *Martini Wisdom*, a humorous collaboration with her daughter based on a recurring Three Tomatoes character. She also wrote the sequel to her first novel, *Can You Hear Us Now*, and is planning to complete the trilogy soon.

Before long, women began asking Cheryl how they could publish their own books. When a friend with a drawerful of essays became her first author, *The Three Tomatoes Book Publishing* was born. Five years later, Cheryl has published over 80 titles, including several audiobooks.

It's one of those things—you follow your gut and see where it takes you. Forcing it doesn't work, but this one obviously has.

The pandemic lockdown brought another unexpected twist: Tomato Cocktails.

I thought about my friends living alone in the city and how isolating it must be.

Cheryl recalls that she invited a few friends to join a Wednesday Zoom cocktail hour—no agenda, just talk about whatever.

She mentioned it in a newsletter and on Facebook, and the group grew organically. A core set of women showed up weekly, forming deep bonds despite many had never met in person.

We became a safe haven. Sometimes someone would break down, but everyone else lifted them back up. Five years later, we're still meeting on Zoom every other week.

Cheryl attributes *The Three Tomatoes'* loyalty to its inclusive spirit—a value rooted in her childhood. Moving frequently as a child, often mid-school year, taught her to notice the person left out and bring them in.

> *That's really how I feel about* The Three Tomatoes:
> *Come on in. I'll make you feel comfortable. Then you'll*
> *meet other people.*

The feedback has been deeply moving.

> *I've had women tell me we changed their lives—that*
> *we gave them a purpose at a time they were giving up.*
> *People want to be seen and heard. We give them that*
> *in a vibrant, fun, engaging way.*

Cheryl's message to women who've withdrawn from life after forty is simple:

> *Put yourself out there. Engage with other people. Join*
> *a group, volunteer, help someone—it gets you out of*
> *your own head.*

Her biggest frustration remains reaching more women.

> *The people who know us are loyal and love it. But we*
> *need more people to know about us. There's a huge*
> *audience out there.*

She's proud of what's been built: a community that celebrates women's vibrancy, defies ageist stereotypes, and keeps trying new things.

> *"We're not about to sit down. If society still looks at*
> *us through an ageism lens, that's not how we see*

And somewhere in the mix, Cheryl knows there's a third and final novel waiting to be written. After all, it's *The Three Tomatoes.*

RANDIE LEVINE-MILLER
The Hostess with the Mostess

This aging thing has been getting to me lately. I never thought about it before, but since the COVID years— all of a sudden, voila! I'm an old broad. Yes, I am—but a great old broad—still out there with enthusiasm, curiosity, and a zest for life.

IN HER MID-SEVENTIES, RANDIE CONTINUES,

I'm living life on my own terms. It would be great if I had a life partner, but as long as I have people in my life who I care about who care about me, I'm fine. Well, at least most of the time. Sometimes I get lonesome. The right man has probably taken a left turn! The problem? The older ones are often downwardly mobile, bitter, or have come out of the closet! I don't want to work at a relationship at this stage of my life. If something were to happen organically, I'd be in for the ride!

Randie believes that dissension creates disease.

When my husband died, and I didn't get what I was entitled to, I let it go. I remembered a couple who fought publicly in court over money, and both died of cancer within a few years of each other. I decided as

*long as I have a comfortable lifestyle and am able to
support myself and donate to causes or help someone
in need, I'm just fine.*

Randie was born to be a performer. That's all she ever dreamed
about, and her parents were very supportive. Even her birth an-
nouncement said, "A star is born." Her mother took her to singing,
acting, and dancing lessons.

At sixteen, she spent the summer at the Gateway Playhouse
in Bellport, Long Island, studying musical theater and acting. She
was a nun in *The Sound of Music.* Earlier, she'd attended Camp
Geneva, a Jewish kids' camp with an astonishing alumni list—Marvin Hamlisch, Penny Marshall, Gary Marshall, and James Caan.
"Moose" Charlap composed *Peter Pan* on the same upright piano
that Marvin later composed original weekly shows for eight weeks
each season. Randie got to sing some of what she considers to be
Marvin's best work. But she says:

> *I wanted to be a Broadway star. I had every
> opportunity, and so many people thought that was
> going to happen, but I screwed up every one of them. I
> suffered from paralyzing stage fright, which is why I
> wound up behind the scenes doing publicity.*

She recalls that when she was studying as a kid, she performed
at Ward's Island.

> *Years later, I heckled an audience when they didn't
> applaud one of my performers. I said, 'You're a
> tough audience. Reminds me of the time I performed
> at Ward's Island for the Criminally Insane.' They
> laughed, and then I had them in the palm of my hand
> after that.*

Randie's career in public relations began with eyebrow-raising assignments—an erotic film festival, books like *The Whole Sex Catalog*, and media pitches involving conversations about oral sex on TV in the 1970s. "It was a different world," she says, laughing.

She went on to represent authors, publishers, and Fortune 500 clients, including Alcoa, Pittsburgh Paints, and General Foods, specializing in getting them on television and radio in literally every city in the United States. For five years, she was the broadcast consultant for *Discover* magazine, as well as the Discover Awards for Technological Innovation, which was held at Epcot. What she was promoting in the '90s, which seemed very sci-fi then, are now our everyday realities.

But when she couldn't book Suzanne Somers' breast doctor on *The View* to discuss breast biopsies after 9/11, she knew it was time to segue to something else.

> *So, what did I do? I went into show business! My passion became my life and has been for the last quarter-century. I wasn't earning a living, but I was truly living!*

For nine years, she produced most of the in-house events at the Friars Club, including celebrity luncheons honoring legendary show business figures, including Jane Powell, Debbie Reynolds, Peter Bogdanovich, Marvin Hamlisch, Tovah Feldshuh, Susan Lucci, Joy Behar, Alan King, Frankie Valli, and Neil Sedaka. She also produced star-studded musical tributes to Broadway icons, including movie producer Marty Richards, with Marvin Hamlisch hosting, as well as accompanying a few performers on the piano; a music tribute to composer Charles Strouse with the best of Broadway; and well-known musical performers saluting songwriter Ervin Drake, as well as other special musical nights honoring Broadway performers.

Randie takes pride in mentoring and inspiring others.

One of my credos is that enthusiasm makes the difference—the big difference, based on a sermon I heard Norman Vincent Peale give over fifty years ago. I believe it keeps me ageless and curious. I've discovered and helped launch several people into what became successful PR careers.

In 2012, Randie started her "Randie's Roundtable," held monthly at Sardi's. The gatherings attract award-winning actors, directors, playwrights, producers, and press agents.

Some of the people I was a fan of as a kid are now my friends. They're great storytellers.

The Roundtable is about camaraderie, not networking.

These afternoons are so special, and we all look forward to being together one day a month. We share stories, we laugh. It's better than therapy, and it's private. Everyone knows that what's said at Sardi's stays at Sardi's.

Randie's Roundtable has been described as a spin-off of the legendary Algonquin Round Table without the snobbery and elitism. The Algonquin Round Table ended after ten years, and Randie's started over thirteen years ago and is still going strong. It's a much sought-after invitation in the show business community.

What brings her joy now?

Connecting with fascinating, joyful, and remarkable people. Seeing a beautiful older couple holding hands, talking to strangers and/or their dogs. Seeing great

*theater and outstanding musical performances.
Hosting, producing, and performing for an
enthusiastic audience.*

*I'm grateful and thank God for every healthy day and
for friendships. I'm very grateful that I have some
authentic exemplary people in my life who care about
me, who I care about. I have no immediate family, and
that truly fills that missing piece in my life.*

She's also learned restraint.

*It's important to be assertive without being
aggressive, to be on time, to be respectful. My
current credo, which was also my late mother's, is
'Expectation is the death of serenity.' I do good things
without expecting thanks—even saved the life of a
woman who'd been horrible to me. Joel Osteen once
said, 'Do something kind for someone who's been
unkind to you.' I did, and it felt good doing that deed.*

Ten years ago, along with Cheryl Benton, she created *Toma-toes Got Talent,* a talent contest for women past forty who may have started out to be professional singers but segued to other careers. As a direct result, several alumni jump-started their careers. Some of them have gotten the prestigious MAC Award as they've gone on to perform regularly.

Randie performed in and emceed the shows. She also wrote *Broadway Babe,* a column which she started during the pandemic that ran for almost five years in The *Three Tomatoes* newsletter, unearthing free entertainment on the Internet and sharing behind-the-scenes stories and anecdotes.

It's very important to wake up with a smile on your face and a sense of purpose. I feel we must have passion, compassion, and enthusiasm for living and be grateful for every day that we remain healthy on this planet!

I'm still evolving and try to be the best person I can be—I'm not done yet!

FRANCENE KATZEN
Turning Hardship into Hope

*Every day is a gift, because I have seven friends that
have lost kids—five to overdoses and two to suicide.
We're one of the lucky ones.*

Francene's life has been shaped by her boundless optimism, her
resilience in adversity, and her commitment to helping others.
Her warmth and cheerfulness seem to come naturally, even after
difficult years supporting her daughter through addiction and recovery.

*It just made my whole week," she says of a small
gesture of kindness, and those who know her see that
sense of gratitude and excitement for life "just comes
out of her pores.*

Her journey has not been an easy one. Francene's early professional life was spent in the mortgage business, working as a loan
processor, closer, and originator.

*I was a terrible originator because I talked too much,
and I couldn't get the deals.*

But she found her place and built a good life with her husband,

Michael, whom she's been married to for over thirty-six years. She reflected on the partnership they forged while raising their daughter.

I thank goodness every day that we have built this life together.

When her daughter reached eighth grade, Francene decided to retire from part-time work to focus on being present at home.

I wanted to make sure she had structure and wasn't getting into drugs and alcohol—just to keep her safe.

But despite her best efforts, her daughter's teenage years brought unexpected challenges:

In ninth grade, we found out she was drinking. By tenth grade, smoking pot. By eleventh grade, she had gotten into heroin.

Francene and Michael fought tirelessly for their daughter's recovery. After multiple treatments, relapses, and setbacks, their daughter eventually graduated from college and started a new life. Her daughter now has an excellent job, a strong relationship, and two delightful children.

Every day is a gift, because I have seven friends who have lost kids—five to overdoses and two to suicide. We're one of the lucky ones.

Francene's gratitude is palpable:

I think it's always been my outlook on life to be grateful for what you have, not worry about what you don't have.

Her daughter's struggle became Francene's mission.

*If she was able to get into recovery and be okay, it was
going to be my mission to educate people on drugs and
alcohol, and try to talk to kids and parents, and help
save any and all children that I could.*

She began speaking at schools, joined nonprofit boards, and
worked with organizations like Substance Abuse Free Environment
to educate sixth graders in her county about addiction and recovery.

*Just because a child makes a mistake doesn't mean it's
the end of their life. We want to give them hope. A lot
of them recover and do very well, and that's what I
say about my own daughter—look at her.*

Francene's approach is rooted in gratitude, faith, and practicality. During the hardest moments, she leaned on friends, her
faith, and even small comforts:

*It was really faith, you know. I turned to God and
said, 'Look, I need some help,' and I would walk and
pray.*

She also credits her circle of friends for helping her and her
daughter rebuild their lives.

*My friends actually became her friends because she
didn't have any friends. We would go to lunch, find
stuff to do—cooking, library, Sweet Mondays. Little by
little, she did it. Once she got out of rehab, the three of
us pretty much did everything together.*

She refuses to indulge in self-pity, focusing instead on what she can do for others.

> *You can either make good out of it, or you can feel*
> *sorry for yourself and go 'why me?' I don't have time*
> *to say that. I've got to help this kid and do my part.*

Her involvement in the book and author community has become a source of joy.

> *During the pandemic, I found Zippy Book Club online.*
> *I like being around other people that I'm going to*
> *learn from and have a lot in common with. Out of this*
> *group, we've all built wonderful friendships—even*
> *though we've never met in person.*

During the pandemic, Francene also discovered The Three Tomatoes, remains an active participant in the Tomatoes' Virtual Cocktail Hour, and contributes a monthly book review to The Three Tomatoes website. She treasures her role as a supporter of authors and friends:

> *There's so much sorrow in this world, but you have to*
> *look for the joy in each day.*

Francene finds pleasure in simple things: playing tennis with friends, reading, being outdoors.

> *I love being outside. I also clean my own house! Or*
> *volunteer. There's always something somebody needs*
> *help with. I don't think life has to be over when your*
> *kids go away and live on their own, or even when you*
> *become a grandparent.*

She's never stopped learning or trying new things, picking up tennis in her forties and encouraging others...

> *...to find a new passion, find a purpose. Life has to*
> *have a purpose and a passion.*

She passes on her lessons in self-reliance to her daughter:

> *I don't care what kind of degree you get; you better*
> *get a job that you can support yourself. Take care of*
> *you.*

Francene's story is also one of generational healing. Her own mother struggled with addiction, and Francene was determined to break the cycle for her daughter.

> *I wanted to make it different and be a different kind of*
> *mom than my mom was.*

She's open about her family's history and the importance of education and vigilance:

> *Now that I've been educated on how addiction works*
> *and it can be passed on, I know you have to watch for*
> *things. We all know a lot more now than we did back*
> *in 2006.*

She also knows how to laugh at life's ironies, telling stories of family quirks and her own love of chocolate:

> *At least chocolate doesn't embarrass me in public!*

Her warmth, humor, and honesty make her an anchor for friends, family, and the community.

Francene's advice for others is practical and encouraging:

> *Pick up a new hobby, try different recipes, read a*

book, make new friends, entertain, garden, volunteer. There are all kinds of things. I don't think life has to be over when your kids go away or even when you become a grandparent.

For Francene, the answer to hardship is always to keep moving forward, to seek out meaning, and to find—or create—joy, no matter what.

It's not what we're dealt, but how we get up and move forward.

HOLLI GERSH
Starting Over at Seventy-Three

I've just blown up my life.

H OLLI GERSH SAYS THIS MATTER-OF-FACTLY.

I've left a long-term relationship, put my Long Island
house on the market, and moved full-time into my
Manhattan apartment. I'm in flux. It's painful—but
incredibly exciting. For the first time in a long while,
I'm asking: Who am I, and what do I want?

Holli's path has never been linear. She studied fashion, art,
and interior design before marrying, raising a daughter, and working as an interior designer. At thirty-six, she divorced, remarrying
two years later to a client—twenty-nine years her senior.

It was an unusual relationship but a remarkable
thirty-year marriage.

Her husband, a former Golden Gloves boxing champion
turned educator and camp owner, drew Holli into his world of real
estate, film investments, and travel.

*He realized I was creative and smart and made me his
partner.*

When he fell ill, she took over their residential rental business, ran it after his death, and eventually burned out. Caregiving, Holli admits, was both exhausting and strangely sweet. She learned to adapt to her husband's changing mental state, sometimes with humor—like the morning she coaxed him into the shower by tap-dancing in her underwear.

It was like Benjamin Button—*he moved backward
through life, and I had to meet him where he was.*

While living in Woodstock, she rediscovered painting and revitalized the local Artists Association, turning it into a state-chartered museum.

*Woodstock has a deep artistic history, and I saw
the potential. Of course, artists are contentious,
but we did it.*

Just before her husband's decline, Holli began collaborating with an independent filmmaker on a script based on his memoir. The project evolved into a more personal story about their marriage and the challenges of dementia caregiving. After her husband's death, she and the filmmaker became romantically involved.

After years of ups and downs, she ended that relationship but remained committed to finishing the film in which she plays herself. They reconciled some time after her interview. They both entered therapy and worked very hard on their relationship. In August 2024, he was diagnosed with stage 4 metastatic pancreatic cancer. This was a death sentence, but he fought valiantly to stay alive. He hoped to still be alive when a cure was found. Unfortunately, he lost that battle on July 29, 2025. Holli was at his side through that terrible year and was there when he died at home, surrounded by loved ones.

Holli reports that she's back to the place she was when we first spoke. Her plan is still the same; it has just been postponed a bit. *"I discovered I'm a pretty good actress,"* she says with a grin.

Today, Holli sits on the boards of NYU Steinhardt's Dean's Council, the Tri-State Maxed Out Women PAC, and *We Care*, which supports survivors of domestic abuse. She has resumed interior design work—recently completing projects in Nashville and Atlantic City—and begun modeling for her friend Gabrielle's fashion line.

Women want to see clothes on bodies that look like theirs. It's been fun to be part of that.

She is also exploring acting, painting, and other creative outlets without the pressure to monetize them.

This phase is about making meaning, not money. If it touches my soul, that's enough.

Learning to prioritize herself is new territory. Recently, when friends invited themselves over for dinner, she surprised herself by saying no.

I felt guilty at first but then realized—this is self-care. I've always been the caregiver. Now, I'm practicing taking care of me.

Holli's political activism runs deep. She has long worked to elect pro-choice women and vividly remembers warning young women in 2019 that Roe v. Wade could be overturned.

They looked at me like I was crazy. Three years later,

here we are.

She is blunt about misogyny, antisemitism, and the divisions among women.

I've already been through junior high—I'm not going back. Madeleine Albright was right: there's a place in hell for women who don't support other women.

The practical challenge ahead is selling the Long Island house.

It's beautiful, but I don't want a country place anymore. I just want to be here in the city.

Letting go of the home—and the life attached to it—is daunting but liberating.

I'm not worried about five years from now. I'm focused on right now—trying new things, exploring, journaling. Sometimes I wake up sad, but then I think: What's going to happen today? I don't know—but it's going to be interesting.

DEBORAH KOENISBERGER
A Heart of Gold and a Mission

There's a lot we can care about.

Dᴇʙᴏʀᴀʜ ɢʀᴇᴡ ᴜᴘ ᴍᴏᴅᴇʟɪɴɢ. Sʜᴇ loved fashion and had a very tight-knit community: family and extended family. After studying languages, she became an interpreter at the United Nations but didn't want to be stuck behind a desk, so she went back to the world of fashion and eventually opened her own store in 1989.

> *I got married in 1990 and had two boys, Florian and*
> *Stephan. So, you know, as a young mom running a*
> *business, being an entrepreneur, all of that, life is very*
> *busy.*

She and the children walked to the shop by way of Madison Square Park, at that time a scary, drug-ridden place.

> *I would take the boys to the playground in the*
> *morning, and then to work. One morning, I noticed*
> *this young woman and a child. She was nineteen*
> *years old, she had a three-year-old daughter, and*
> *they were sleeping in a cargo box because she had no*

*other options. She was molested at home, left home,
and then went into a shelter where she was further
molested. And she decided she was going to just take
her chances on the dirt.*

*Where I came from, that world doesn't exist. There's
no world in which somebody would never have a
couch, pull-out chair, or a rug somewhere that I could
sleep on and not just be under the elements. So, I was
quite shocked.*

After a few days, the young woman disappeared. The memory
was part of what Deborah calls the trifecta that changed her life.
Part two was meeting Bobbi Brown, then a budding makeup artist,
while on vacation.

*I ran into her, and we had a conversation. She's like,
listen, when you go back to New York, I'm going to
come visit your store. You know, you're a stylist, and
I do makeup, and I've been doing workshops at a
shelter, giving the moms products, and teaching them
how to wear makeup.*

*Let's do something together where you can talk to
them about what to wear. We did our workshop, and
it was amazing. Now, I didn't know anything about
shelters. So, when I went there with Bobbi, I was like,
what is this place? And she explained it to me, and I
met the director.*

Then I noticed that there were kids running around. I

*said, why are there kids? And she said, it's for moms
and their kids. A lot of them are running away from
domestic violence, or whatever the circumstances
that they find themselves homeless, and they're in
these shelters. It's a respite center where they can go
from the danger they were in as a steppingstone to
permanent housing.*

The third part of the trifecta grew out of her lifetime addiction to Stevie Wonder and his lyrics. She never misses a concert. At a 1994 concert, *Conversation Peace*, she was captivated by one song.

It's called Take the Time Out. *It says, take the time
out to love someone, reach your arms out and love
someone, be it a king or some homeless one. We are
one underneath the sun.*

*And it just woke me up, and I was like, okay. I grew
up in a family of service. My parents were always
helping someone. People were coming home with my
mom from church; she was always cooking as if the
army was coming to dinner and passing food out. And
my dad, multiple times in the week, would be the only
one pulling over to bail somebody out and dig them
out, or jumpstart their car, or whatever.*

*I grew up with that kind of service. You know, you
always work trying to help someone. So, I heard the
words. The young woman in the park, Stevie's song,
the meeting with Bobbi was just all, like, wow, and it
just swept me away.*

Deborah went back to the shelter and asked what they did for Christmas. They didn't have more than ninety-nine cents, so they were going to the dollar store to get each child a ninety-nine-cent present. Christmas was a big deal in her family, so she asked if she could adopt Christmas that year. There were about 135 kids and some ninety moms.

So, I got all the names, all the ages, all the genders of the kids, and I got each child a stuffed animal, a book, and a little accessory, like a scarf, gloves. I rented a U-Haul, and I got food catered. We had an incredible celebration with the moms and the kids, except for the one moment that almost marred it all, where one mom said to her daughter, who was so excited and went to show her mom what she got, and she was like, 'So? Ain't nobody has done nothing for me.' What I learned was that they'd never had it, so they couldn't appreciate it for their children. So, note to self.

Easter was also a big deal when she was a child, so she asked if she could do Easter. This time, she knew she had to include the mothers, so she asked Ivanka Trump, who had a costume jewelry line on a home shopping network, and got 90 pieces of jewelry. Bobbi Brown contributed beauty products.

We made a gift bag for the moms, so when the Easter Bunny called up the child's name, the mom came with, and the child had their Easter basket, and the mom got her gift bag.

And I want to think of Hearts of Gold as the heartbeat in that flatline that would just take them up out of that,

*whatever, for those moments, and just erase some
of the bad memories, and replace it with something
good that says, somebody cares about you, somebody
loves you, and here you are. I'm somebody who sees
you and values you. So, that is how Hearts of Gold got
started. And now, it's thirty-one years later, and over
40,000 moms helped.*

*I never looked back. It just kept growing, and then
people from the community got involved, and I had
my boutique, so I had a lot of customers, and they
started to help me.*

Deborah opened her boutique, Noir et Blanc, on September 5, 1989. Then came Hearts of Gold. Her customers and friends kept trying to give her things for the moms. They didn't need dress clothes—they needed things to wear every day—a pair of jeans or whatever, so when she opened a thrift store, she decided to take all that stuff from customers who were willing to give it to her, and she spent about two years amassing enough to open a thrift store – TTH, The Thrifty Hog, because who heard of a thrifty hog? It was so catchy.

*I'm in a space where all three entities exist: the
boutique, the thrift and vintage stores, and Hearts of
Gold offices. We use all of the space, so in this 6,000
square foot space, we hire moms and their adult
children, and give them job training skills, help them
build a resume, pay them a living wage, and help them
qualify for the voucher that they need to get out of
shelter into permanent housing. So, all of that happens
here at 40 West 25th Street. And everything in the*

thrift vintage store is donated by just everyone, and designers as well, and so that's where all that money goes, to pay for the programs and the costs of running the organization.

Initially, Deborah thought that she'd be able to fix the problem.

Why are we having a nineteen-year-old sleeping in a park in New York City? One of the wealthiest cities in the world. It's no one's priority, clearly.

She pointed to the need for job programs and existing housing that would be at least $2,500 less expensive than shelter housing.

It's just insane to me. It makes no sense. So you know, you realize that if somebody really cared, they could fix this. This is fixable. This is absolutely fixable. So that's my conundrum, because I thought by now, we would have just a very different situation.

And I didn't realize that it was like the canals in Amsterdam. You plug one hole, but it's spewing out of the other twenty. And so, I've just made my peace with doing what I can, affecting change where I can, and infusing positivity and love into the lives that we get to touch.

She asks everyone to do whatever they can, no matter how small it may seem.

Lead with kindness. That means check on your neighbor. You have an elderly neighbor; go check on your neighbor. Charity does begin at home—it should.

*This is a model for doing this; we do it, and then other
people follow. So, I say to people of a certain age,
you have time. And in your community, whether it's
through a church or religious organization, if you
want to find something to do, you will find something
to do, because it's right there.*

*Look for somewhere to help—whatever you're
interested in, whatever you love—you love animals,
go find a shelter. Care about each other, care about
humanity, care about why you're here. You didn't
come here to get up every day and make the world a
more miserable place than it is.*

*I'm just saying, there are no such things as small acts
of kindness.*

Part 4

PERFORMERS AND THEATER-CENTRIC CAREERS

Pam Hamilton is a musician, singer, and teacher who has been involved with music since childhood.

Blondell Cummings was a quiet member of a networking group I was part of. We never knew that she was an internationally renowned dancer, choreographer, and filmmaker.

KT Sullivan is a well-known cabaret singer who also heads the Mabel Mercer Foundation and the Dutch Treat Club. She regularly appears at the Algonquin and joins her sister and mother performing on cruise ships.

Pat Addiss started her second career at seventy. She's still producing plays and is planning for worldwide productions of her favorite, *Desperate Measures*. She also co-created the YaYas, a lunch group that brings together interesting women and a program supporting young women in the theater.

Carol Ostrow has had a varied and colorful career performing and producing, including becoming a Las Vegas showgirl at age seventeen.

Magda Katz credits her love of the performing arts, especially theater, to a relative in Budapest, who took her to cafes, concerts, and theater every summer in her childhood. Her career covers a wide span, including being a stage mother and serving as entertainment director at The Lambs.

Merrill Stone, at one point in her career, was known as the crooning gerontologist. She has been a theater and music producer and is still performing at events, including *The Power of Women's Voices*.

PAM HAMILTON
A Life in Many Keys

It's like I'm multi-lingual, but with instruments.

Pᴀᴍ's ᴍᴜsɪᴄᴀʟ ᴊᴏᴜʀɴᴇʏ ɪs ᴏɴᴇ continuous path of *bricolage*—creating from whatever is at hand. When a battered old piano appeared in her home, she taught herself to play, piecing together her first composition at age eleven.

> *It was the day John Kennedy was assassinated. I didn't know how to play, but I composed a kind of requiem. I wanted to capture how happy this man made the world, and how crestfallen we were once he was gone.*

That piano became a place of solace and joy until, one day, she came home to find it in the backyard – chopped into pieces by her father.

> *As a child, I thought it was my fault. That was my musical trauma. It still surfaces.*

And yet, she kept playing.

From her earliest years, Pam was a natural singer. She picked up the violin at eight, guitar at twelve, and soon was performing at church, on local television, and at community concerts.

It's like I'm multi-lingual, but with instruments.

By junior high, she added flute and viola, learning to read music, and continued broadening her skills. The political and cultural turbulence of the 1960s shaped her musical sensibilities.

I listened to Peter, Paul, and Mary, Joan Baez, Judy Collins...all the ladies making that kind of music. I was like a baby hippie. Music was my solace. I couldn't go out and march, but I could write songs about peace, about the end of war.

Black families experienced a great deal of trauma at that time, and Pam faced racism and bullying while being bused to predominantly white schools. She used her music for resilience and hope.

By resilience, or just believing life could be better, I thought I could contribute somehow to the peace effort—by touching people's hearts with my smile, my musings, and my songs. It began for me with that song, 'Let there be peace on earth, and let it begin with me.' That's always been my goal.

After high school, Pam's career blossomed. She signed a record deal, toured with an R&B group, played jazz festivals, and worked in musical theater. Cleveland grew too small for her ambitions—she set her sights on Broadway.

Her father, before his death, surprised her with advice she resisted at the time:

*He told me I should become a teacher—that I'd make a
great teacher.*

Pam laughs at the memory.

I knew that was something I'd never do.

She was wrong.

While touring with a gospel group, a friend mentioned that a
conservatory in Queens desperately needed a violin teacher. Pam
had just come off the road and agreed to try.

*I had never taught a day in my life. I said, 'Give me a
book.' With the little kids, I made games to cover up
the fact that I didn't know what the heck I was doing.
And it worked.*

Soon, more offers followed: the Holland School of the Arts,
Riverbank State Park, and eventually the Harlem Children's Zone,
where she was asked to start an after-school strings program.

*They had all these violins and nobody to teach them.
I said, 'Okay, I'll do that.' Eighteen years later, I'm
still there. I've watched some of my second graders
graduate from high school and still play violin.*

What began as a stopgap became a vocation. Pam had stepped
into her father's prophecy.

When the pandemic shut down her program, Pam kept learning. She became certified in the Mark O'Connor method, which
blends fiddling, gospel, and jazz improvisation. She began coaching
violists in jazz and improv, broadening her students' sense of possibility.

Today, Pam continues to teach part-time. She also performs

with the Pamela Hamiton Duo, and classical and jazz orchestras, at venues from New York's Carnegie Hall and Lincoln Center to Paris' Le Duc Jazz Club.

Her success, she insists, is rooted not only in talent but in resilience—the ability to turn pain into music, setbacks into new directions, and opportunities into lifelong callings. 'Don't you understand? I'm not a teacher,' she once told herself.

But I am a teacher.

Pam's story is one of survival, creativity, and transformation. From that first improvised requiem on a broken piano to teaching generations of young musicians, she has lived her life in many keys.

Her music is both personal and universal—a testament to what is possible when art becomes a refuge, a resistance, and a gift to others.

My goal has always been peace. To touch people's hearts so they hear themselves reflected in my songs. That's what music is for me. That's what keeps me going.

BLONDELL CUMMINGS
Internationally renowned dancer, choreographer, and filmmaker

It's the beauty in things that we sometimes lose track of.

WE KNEW BLONDELL AS AN unassuming woman who always brought her own popcorn to our meetings and spoke mostly about swimming at the Y, with occasional references to judging competitions for grants. It wasn't until our one meeting in her apartment, close to her death, that she spoke openly about having spent much of her time in Paris and needing to track down the many videos she had created of dancers, including herself.

Over ten years after Blondell's death in 2015, I searched the internet to see if I could learn more about her. My first surprise was that she had been a founding member of the dance company of my distant cousin, Meredith Monk. The biggest surprise was the scope and depth of Blondell's work. Most of what follows is adapted from Wikipedia, supplemented by an article from *The Los Angeles Times.*

Born in South Carolina, Blondell spent her childhood in Harlem and her adolescence in Queens. Wikipedia says that "She is known for her experimental choreography and was a fixture in the

New York and Harlem dance scene for decades."

Her education focused on her art, following her BA in dance and education from NYU with a master's in fine arts from Lehman College, before studying at the Martha Graham School of Contemporary Dance.

Blondell created the Cycle Arts Foundation to promote interdisciplinary collaboration and served as an artist-administrator for the Cultural Council Foundation CETA Artists Project while choreographing and dancing her own pieces.

This quote comes from an article in *The Los Angeles Times*: "It's the beauty in things that we sometimes lose track of," wrote choreographer, dancer, and video artist Blondell Cummings (1944–2015) almost thirty years ago. "When I'm at my worst, I don't see it. When I'm at my best, I see it all around me."

Blondell was also known for her pioneering work in exploring and testing the boundaries of filming dancers. She had been trying to collect and catalogue her films during her final illness.

Blondell is one of three women who have passed on and are included in this collection. While the others are included in a later chapter, I've chosen to place her with the entertainers. She was well-known in the dance world, but less so outside that environment. I wanted her to have her place among this group of women in tribute to her talent.

KT SULLIVAN
Singing Through the Years

I was singing before I remember—I can't remember not singing.
My mother was a singer, and I was singing with my brother
at four in church, and I played the piano.

KT, Elizabeth Sullivan's oldest daughter, is a well-known cabaret singer. She frequently appears at the famed Algonquin Hotel in New York City and joins her sister performing on cruise ships.

She loves her life—traveling and singing. She was in London for her seventieth birthday. During COVID, she learned to accompany herself. She loves being able to travel alone, playing for herself, although it requires

getting better at accompanying myself. I'm just
having the best time.

She describes her long-running Algonquin shows as "a party every Friday." Performed without microphones in the historic salon once home to Dorothy Parker and the Round Table, these evenings become gatherings of friends and often include sing-alongs. Her deep connection to music and storytelling found its home in cabaret.

I studied opera and Shakespeare, but cabaret found

me. That's where I could tell stories—mine and the audience's.

KT moved to Los Angeles at twenty-one, where she did commercials and musicals like *Brigadoon* and *Gentlemen Prefer Blondes*. She's done performances of Broadway shows with Roberta Peters in St. Louis. Other performances include municipal opera, *Brigadoon, Carousel,* and *Gentlemen Prefer Blondes* on Broadway in '89 and in '95. But her greatest joy comes from performing in little cabaret rooms.

That's where I really communicate. People empathize with the songs—love, loss, memory. We find common threads.

She finds power in lyrics and quotes Noel Coward's *Bittersweet*: "In my heart will ever lie, just the echo of a sigh. Goodbye."

It's therapy. Memories are bittersweet, and we need to relive them.

KT had been splitting her time between New York and Charlottesville, where her husband had a home. She bought a home there when her husband went into hospice. After her husband passed, KT kept close to his five children and seven grandchildren in Charlottesville, where she now visits monthly.

They lost their mother thirty years ago. They're orphans, and they need me.

KT's love for cabaret also extends to mentoring the next generation through the Mabel Mercer Foundation, which she now leads. Donald Smith, who was Mercer's manager, started the Mabel Mercer Foundation. Mabel received the Medal of Freedom from

Ronald Reagan before she died. Smith wanted people to remember her after she died. People called her a jazz singer over the past two years, but she really wasn't a jazz singer. She was a cabaret singer who performed in intimate settings.

My mother wrote a song about the things that Mabel Mercer did! Frank Sinatra said everything you knew about phrasing you learned from Mabel Mercer. My mother wrote, 'As we dig deep inside to find the joy, to feel the pain they bring.' That's what Mabel did with lyrics.

Donald Smith asked me if the Foundation should go on after him. I said yes. I didn't see myself as an administrator, but I love the songs and the singers.

She proudly speaks of their annual Cabaret Convention— the only one in the world—and their scholarship competition for high schoolers. She speaks about a cover of the New Yorker in 2020, during the pandemic, with a wonderful photo shoot downstairs in front of the office, right there on Ninth Avenue, with no traffic because it was COVID— the worst of COVID. And then they made the cover of the Art Section in The Times. It's five young singers, and they come from the professional art schools around the city. It's all scholarship-based people who really need it. The winner also gets to sing at the Convention. There's lots of excitement about that.

I was so excited about young people on the stage, and those young kids from the high schools in the audience. We give free seats to high school students, and they get excited about these songs. Once they hear them, they get excited; they don't know what they don't know.

Then, once they've heard them and once they've seen them, they see the response like a little girl gets up and says, "Don't Rain on My Parade," and she can see how her peers are just going crazy. This gets them excited because these songs have middles, beginnings, and ends.

She tells a story about one contest:

There was a little boy who won the contest in Durango—he's fifteen. He walked out there and sang, smiled, and broke our hearts. I was sitting next to Rex Reed, and he was in tears. So, this is who we are. Mabel Mercer's Foundation is about the future. We want to make sure that young people do hear these songs and sing them for the rest of their lives.

She entered a new chapter after her husband's death. She's singing on cruises with her sister and mother. Her sister does the big room, and KT does the small room. She puts together groups of people so that she gets a free cruise and says it feels like a high school reunion.

We go on a cruise once a year. We take a lot of women on the cruise, and they have great fun with me in the small room and with my sister in the big room, seeing the world. It's great to be able to see the world. Every year I choose a cruise, someplace I haven't been.

KT's life is rich with travel, yoga, art, and connection.

Friends are so important. After COVID, we realized again how vital that is.

She continues to perform, travel, and embrace this chapter.

*There's a longer life when you're sitting at the piano.
I'm enjoying it so much.*

PAT ADDISS
Reinventing Life, One Stage at a Time

I started a new career when I was seventy years old.
If you want to do the math... don't.

Her initial career shift came decades earlier, after her marriage ended.

I had wanted five children and one adopted child,
but I married the wrong Catholic. After ten years, he
confessed he didn't like children or married life—and
he became a deadbeat ex. Suddenly, I was supporting
three kids in New York City.

Pat insisted on giving her children the best education she could.

They all went to Grace Church School, the most
ecumenical school in New York at the time. I love my
kids, and I love being a mom—but I also like working.
It's good for your ego at any age if you're successful.

With a degree in costume design and merchandising, Pat launched a promotions company—putting corporate logos on everything from tote bags to aprons. They put corporate names on every kind of widget you can imagine. She ran the company for thirty years before handing it to her daughter, a lawyer who wanted to spend more time with her son.

That freed Pat to chase a dream: producing Broadway shows.

You have no idea how difficult it is. Saying it and doing it are two different things—but I'm glad I did it.

She took the Commercial Theater Institute course, graduated, and dove in.

When you graduate from anything, you think you know everything. You know nothing, thankfully.

Her first production was *Little Women* with Sutton Foster.

I never looked back.

Pat went on to produce an eclectic mix: *Buyer and Seller, Spring Awakening, 39 Steps, Gigi*, one of her favorites—which, she says, should have won awards but didn't. She's collected several Tonys along the way, though awards aren't her motivation.

I love theater. The creation. My favorite show of all time is Desperate Measures. *It was a love fest every night—everyone adored each other. It won a lot of awards along the way, including two Drama Desk Awards. It's just an amazing show.*

When the original run was forced to close, Pat refused to let it die. She bought the rights, struck tough deals, and kept pushing.

If I like something, I do it. I'm not a pros-and-cons person. I'm intuitive. I'm also known for my honesty—

don't ask my opinion if you don't want it.

Today, *Desperate Measures* is licensed worldwide, with dozens of productions planned.

Pat's energy spills far beyond Broadway. She co-founded, with Magda Katz, "YaYa," a roundtable for women—born from a reunion with two old Finch College friends.

> *We decided on eleven women at a round table, all there to help each other. Older women mentoring younger women in every way possible. I think that's very important.*

The group meets when schedules allow, and many members have become close friends or collaborators.

> *It's wonderful to see people connect and work together. Very fulfilling.*

Pat also speaks to women over fifty about reinventing themselves.

> *I discovered this focus after I had swallowed a piece of Saran Wrap and couldn't breathe. I went to the NYU Langone Emergency Room, and they started to work on me. I could hear people saying that I was dying. There were all these machines, and all I could do was use my brain. At that time, I was winning The Three Tomatoes' Woman of Purpose award, and I had to think about what a Woman of Purpose was.*

> *I decided that my purpose was to be an inspiration to women over fifty. So many think their life is over,*

but you can do anything. There are all sorts of things you can do—work with charities, raise money for charities, visit shut-ins, etc.

A lot of women get stuck after fifty—COVID made it worse. But we have one life. We know what we have here, so we have to live it. You're never too old—well, maybe for bungee jumping. I feel very strongly that you have only one life to live, and it's up to each of us to live it because you're dead for a long time.

She recalls her aunt, who at age eighty was working in a jewelry store and was called "the old lady" by a customer.

She was so put out she started dyeing her hair red— and did until the day she died. She was a role model for me: keep living, keep going.

Pat says that you must follow your dreams:

People will tell you that you're too old, too fat— whatever. Don't listen! If you don't follow your dream, you'll always live with regrets. Live life on your own terms, not what others tell you. People are quick to give advice, but they don't wake up with you in the morning.

Pat was honored with the Oral History Award from the League of Professional Theatre Women. When her award was presented:

I walked onstage to a standing ovation—I cried. Roma Torre interviewed me about my life, from childhood on. My daughter had dug up so much about me I didn't even remember. It was overwhelming and wonderful.

What makes her happiest?

Being with my friends. Going to the theater. Creating. New York has an energy no other place has. During lockdown in Virginia, I was well cared for but creatively dead—no one spoke my language.

This winter:

I'll go back with a different attitude. I'll work with the local community theater. You can't just sit and say, 'Poor me.' You have to do something.

Pat believes the secret to resilience is relationships.

Your girlfriends are the ones who keep you going. It's important to have good friends—and to be one. Casual acquaintances are the icing. Friends are the cake.

CAROL OSTROW
Performer, Director, Author

*I do a lot of things, happily. Never get bored. I've been an actress,
a dancer, choreographer, a producer who puts everything
together, and a director, so I never get bored. There's always
something for me to get in trouble with, and lately I have been
writing poetry. So, it's a full life, as long as I keep my strength up,
which I'm always worried about.*

CAROL EXPLAINED THAT SHOW BUSINESS is really all she knows, because of her beautiful and talented mother, who never got the opportunity to be a dancer, which she always wanted to do. She had a family, and she had to work with her husband, who was in the restaurant business. When Carol was two years old and dancing around in diapers, her mother thought, maybe, maybe her daughter has a little talent.

She went to Anne's Dance Studio in Brooklyn, New York, at two years old, where she sang and danced, and loved it, with the audience applauding her.

> *It was love, and I never got over that feeling. I can be
> so nervous getting on the stage today, I could throw
> my guts up, and then when I get up on that stage, I
> forget the whole thing, and I'm absolutely in heaven.
> I just love emoting and expressing myself, even with
> other people's words.*

*I just find it a wonderful experience. So that's what I
do, but I can tell you there was a time, about ten years
ago, I'd written a show, directed it, choreographed it,
and starred in it. It was at our country club. I'm not a
member anymore, but that's how I could make myself
comfortable with this club, by doing all their shows.*

*And so, it was very hard to get everybody into
rehearsals. It was a fun show, an easy show, but
they had dancing routines, and I couldn't get them
away from tennis, golf, and lunch. They didn't want
to rehearse. I was a wreck, so I kept searching them
out, rehearsing them, and I didn't rehearse my own
lines, because I was going to be the narrator, getting
up there, introducing the act, and I had one little thing
that I was going to do. And I got up there, and I forgot
my lines.*

*I was the only one. Mind you, the only professional
who forgot her lines, and it just did something to me
that I'm never going to do this to myself again.*

So, for ten years, she would write shows, or get a show, and
raise the money for it, put it on Broadway, or off-Broadway. She did
it with partners, she did it alone.

And, lately, she's gotten back into the joy of acting, not because she felt confident; it was a hurdle that she pushed herself to
get past.

*And once again, before performing, I throw up. I
think, what am I doing to myself? Do I need this? And
then I get up there, and it's wonderful, and I love it.*

Carol was a Las Vegas showgirl. She ran away from home when she was seventeen because her mother kept putting her in beauty contests—her dream, not Carol's. She ran away from home with a magician, whom she married, and they went to Las Vegas. And in Las Vegas, she divorced him.

She started really enjoying show business, but it was a tough life. She wanted to become a choreographer, not just someone up there moving around the stage. There was nothing wrong with being a showgirl, and in the time that she did it, they were glorified. They made women look magnificent with lights and makeup, and if you saw the girls without the makeup, they weren't gorgeous.

*I worked for a wonderful choreographer, Don Arden.
I learned to be a choreographer by watching, taking
lessons, and being very careful about not pulling
muscles, which I did all the time. It was so difficult to
be a dancer, and I'm very tall and not meant to be a
little skinny girl in the line. I learned a great deal, but
to earn a little extra money, I became what was called
the swing girl. I learned everybody's part.*

She was a Don Arden dancer at the Desert Inn Hotel and met some of the most incredible stars, who were very kind to her. Years later, when she became the president of the Actors' Temple, producing their fundraisers, improving the place, raising money, and doing all the things that she'd been training to do, she would see pictures on the walls of those people that she worked with in Las Vegas—Milton Berle, The Barry Sisters.

So, fast forward, there was Las Vegas. There were three marriages, and all the time I worked. I was even a high-fashion model when there was no show business, when I moved to Washington, D.C., with husband number two.

She lost weight; became a high-fashion model, and started choreographing the shows that she was in. She found the shows dull; the girls looked like bored human hangers. She decided to teach them how to move and moved along with them in the show to make a little extra money, learned the right lighting, and put on some "pretty damn good shows," all for charity.

She left Washington, D.C., to marry her third husband in New York. She didn't know what to do next because she was too old to model. She decided to take acting lessons again and go to Broadway and off-Broadway. She didn't have Broadway credits, so nobody took her seriously.

Well, if they're not going to take me seriously, I'm going to buy a show that's right for me. I'm going to raise the money and put myself in it.

Which I did, and it was the worst show you've ever seen in your life. It was not at all what I'd hoped for, but it was my first attempt.

My life has been a series of lucky breaks, being in the right time, at the right place, and making things happen because I was too stupid to be too afraid, or

whatever you want to attribute it to. I took a chance.
I didn't know that I wouldn't make it somehow,
because my mother had given me that confidence that
no matter what I do, even if I failed, I'd learn good
lessons and somehow make it work!

A famous producer saw this terrible show. She called him up by accident and introduced herself, and he said, "Was that your terrible show that I saw the other night?"

And I was so embarrassed. He said, 'Look, don't be
embarrassed. I'm going to teach you how to produce.'

He was actually interested in her raising money, which she learned to do. It stood her in very good stead for producing, which was her karma.

And that's how I learned, from failure to success to
failure to success, success, success, and failure again.

She began producing shows with Arthur Cantor. Very few said no to him because he told the truth. He said, "I can't guarantee that this is going to be a hit, but it's a wonderful show, and you're going to be proud of it, and you're going to call it your show." And people believed him, and they invested. Half the time it paid back, half the time it did not. You must never promise what you can't deliver.

I started producing with zest and joy and had some
pretty good shows off-Broadway. I did Bo Jest. I did
Ann Meara's very first show called After-Play, *with her*
husband, Jerry Stiller. She was brilliant and became a
lifelong friend. I loved her dearly, respected her talent,
and met many other stars who worked for me.

And then, my husband passed away. My parents passed away. My brother, my only sibling, passed away, and I was alone. I had friends, but every single person in my family—cousins, second cousins, third cousins—gone, and at young ages, too.

And I thought, 'What am I going to do with my life?' So, a friend of mine in show business said, 'Go to the Actor's Temple. The Actor's Temple is a great place, a little shabby, but you'll find it home.'

She walked into that place and saw the pictures of people that she had worked with! All of these stars!

It boggled my mind, all of these magnificent human beings, who were very famous because of their talent.

The Actor's Temple was very shabby. The ceiling had just caved in on Yom Kippur, of all times. This place needed her skills.

I have the ability to raise money and put on shows! Let's put on a show! And I did. And I used my skills to the best advantage to raise money to keep this magnificent place alive. It's 108 years old and always needs something. I mean, what doesn't at 108 years old need repair constantly?

I found a home to do the things that I love, which is produce shows, be with the people in show business that I adore, and work with the best board that anyone could ever work with, because they never say no. They just say, 'Go for it, Carol, go for it!' And I do, and I drive myself crazy and keep working!

*I love meeting new people. I adore meeting new
people—good people—that I surround myself with.
And I have the best girlfriends anyone could ask for,
many of whom are published poets and writers. And
I adore Cheryl, who is our Head Tomato at The Three
Tomatoes Publishing. And there's a whole new group
of friends right there.*

*I invite them to things, they invite me, and it's an ever-
growing circle of friends. Of course, you can't spread
yourself too thin. I have my opera pals, and that's
very important to me. I adore opera. It has everything
in it: drama, music, costumes. Everything you can
experience in the theater is in opera.*

*I'm very controlling. That's my training. As an actor,
you have to control yourself. As a director, you have
to control what's going on. And as a producer, you
have to control everything but allow people to be
who they are. You cannot be the director, the lighting
person, and the customer. You have to gather all of
these talented people to work with you and trust their
talent."*

During 2020, COVID closed Broadway. She'd been producing, and everything shut down. She still had to raise money for the
synagogue, so she started learning how to make videos about the
lives of those who came to the synagogue in the very beginning, like
the Barry Sisters, the Three Stooges, and the Marx Brothers. She

made about eight videos and was really excited, and again was in this creative mode and couldn't shut herself down.

> *But I needed more expression. I love to write. All of a sudden, I thought of a rhyming story that I was going to send to a friend as a birthday gift. I wanted to remember my friends, so I wrote this funny little ditty about this friend that I called Shitty. And it was funny! It really was funny, and I thought, gee, this is great, I'm going to wile away my time with rhyme. And I did. I came out with about 100 poems. I would send them to my friends.*

She kept writing poems and sent them to friends. One friend said, "Why don't you get this published?" She found The Three Tomatoes, and they published her first book. She wrote a second book, which was published about a year ago. She's got about fifty more poems ready to be published.

"I just can't stop it. It's a spigot. It won't turn off. I've even gotten into lyrics, and that is a challenge. I can be depressed like everybody else, but I don't want to write that. Most of my poetry is about being uplifted. Oh, don't be down. You can get your way up. And I like to do something funny at the end."

And with that, she rattled off a poem:

> *Wanting to expand on my creativity,*
> *Becoming the actual, factual reality that I try to get*
> *into each day.*
> *Sometimes exhausting, but be that as it may,*
> *thinking becomes an activity du jour,*
> *digging down for something so pure that no one has*
> *ever done before.*

Perhaps a disease I can find a cure.
Dream on, I say to myself. Have faith in the ideas I put
on a shelf.
Right now, I cannot get out of bed.
All these ideas swirling in my head.
Well, right now, I'll just get out of my comfortable bed,
stop thinking, and do something original instead:
get some ice cream and forget the whole damn thing."

I aspire to be better—loving, kind, and giving. We
all get into ruts, and the best thing is to get help. And
that's what you do, and what I admire so much. You're
there giving a helping hand.

You've got to do it yourself. No one can do it for you.
When you get out of bed, take that bath, brush your
teeth, comb your hair, slap on the makeup, and face
the world. Come what may, you face the world. And
that's how I look at it. Every day is an adventure.

Carol has a new boyfriend. She met him in the laundry room. She says it's a miracle that they found each other because she surely wasn't looking, and neither was he. She met two husbands and another boyfriend in an elevator.

I have a gratitude book that really helps me. I start off
saying I am grateful to be alive. I am grateful to have
the opportunity to pay my bills and buy food. Not
everybody can do that.

It's very important to me to be of service. Whatever

I have, whatever gifts I have, thank you, God. But I do want to share it with other people. Gifts are to be shared, and I'm the luckiest girl in the world. I knock on wood, chase away the bad spirits, whatever you want to do, but I feel God gave me many gifts, and I want to share them, because you can't keep them. We've got to share them and have beauty, share beauty, give beauty. Be kind, be gentle, and do the best you can.

And forgive yourself if you've done something stupid or unkind, because you can always say, 'I'm sorry,' and mean it.

MAGDA KATZ
Saying Yes to Opportunities

I was born in Hungary, the only child of Holocaust survivors.
They'd both been married, lost their spouses, so I was the hope
of the future for them. They were very hardworking;
they worked all the time, so I was left alone a lot of times
or with somebody as a little child.

THEY ESCAPED HUNGARY IN 1956, came to the U.S., and life was extremely hard. Magda's escape was her imagination. It took her out of any situation. She would sit in class, not knowing a word of English, and just daydream. It was always about theater, about the arts, and the people around her were just not the kind of people she wanted to be with.

But every summer, from the time she was four, her mother would send her to Budapest to stay with a very cultured relative who grew up in Berlin. She had a huge influence on Magda and took her to cafes and theaters and introduced her to the art world. That planted a seed in her that never left.

She had a bad experience in sixth grade. She was just starting to learn English and asked for a pencil—first day of school—and the teacher said, "You're talking! Get back!" She put her at a table by herself, and nobody was supposed to talk to her for a whole year.

Just because there were no immigrant kids then, and
my parents didn't speak enough English to go up and

say, 'This is not what you do to a child,' and they were
from a culture where the teacher was always right.

That gave her a lot of time to sit there and escape with her
imagination. She had a movie in her head all the time, because she
had to entertain herself.

*Nobody was talking to me; nobody was relating to
me. And then I said to myself, I need to have friends.*

Her father would take her ice skating on Sundays, and she
thought that if she befriended one of the popular boys and said, "I'm
going skating," other kids would come. Sure enough, he brought
all these friends. She would skate with them all the time, but they
weren't friendly at school.

*If I wanted to create anything for myself, I had to
organize. I had to create it. I didn't fit into the square;
I had to make my own circle.*

She was miserable in junior high school. She and her mother
were watching Milton Berle on TV, and he mentioned that he went
to the Professional Children's School.

*And I said to my mother in Hungarian, 'You know,
he went to a special school for actors.' So, my mother
says, 'You call them tomorrow and see if you could go
there, because I think you'll be happier.'*

*So, I called Professional Children's School (in New
York City). I got in. And I went there. It was like, oh, I
could breathe, you know. I was around these fabulous
people. I mean, really, they were on Broadway; they*

were here.

Her mother didn't want her going out of town for college. She was sure that she could get into Finch College. At first, they didn't take her, and then she went back and said, "I really, really want to come here." And they took her.

If you say no to me, it's like, ugh, I've really got to do it. So, I went, and I really liked it. I made some nice friends there.

She's still friendly with some people from Finch.

I was able to go to the theater. I was able to go to the Met. We had classes in the Met. It was a wonderful, wonderful school, because a lot of the teachers were from Columbia University. They were moonlighting there, so we had all the best teachers.

My mother said to me, if you want to meet somebody, you've got to meet them doing a sport or something. So, she said, "Why don't you go skiing?" So, I started going skiing.

I got into a terrible car accident on the way to the mountain. I had a head-on collision with the truck, and I ended up in the hospital. I got a broken jaw. When I was bandaged up, I said, 'Please do not call my parents. I want to call them, because if they hear somebody calling that I'm in the hospital, my mother will collapse.' Because that was her only thing to live for. So, I called them, and I said, 'Look, I'm okay. I got

*into a car accident.' My father got in the car and drove
eight hours up to Vermont to get me.*

That was in '69, her last year of college. After her jaw healed,
her mother said that she could go skiing again, but she would have
to take the bus that left from the local ski shop. The bus broke down,
and she started talking to another girl.

*This girl in front of me says, 'Oh, I belong to a ski
house. How are we going to get up there?' I said,
'Come to my house, convince my mother, and we'll
take the car up.' So, we drove up, and lo and behold, in
the house was my future husband. Is that something?
So, I really believe sometimes bad things happen for
good reasons. We met, and we got to like each other
quite fast. We got engaged within three months, and
we got married within six months.*

*My mother is old-fashioned. 'He's got to marry you;
he's got to marry you.' She said to my husband-to-be,
'Listen, I don't know what your intentions are, but
she's going to Europe for the summer, so, you know,
maybe you'll see her after the summer.' And then he
asked me to marry him, so we got married before the
summer.*

She needed a job at that time. The parents of a friend from
Finch owned a restaurant on Broadway called McGinnis's, where
all the stars used to go. At school one day, she told me that she and
her parents were invited to a party for a very famous producer. He
owned Embassy Pictures, and he said to her, "If you need a job,
come up to my office. I'm sure we'll find you something."

She says, 'I don't want to work in show business.'
I said, 'Well, I do.' Next day, I phoned Embassy
Pictures. I said to them, 'I understand there might
be an opening. Could I come up?' They said, 'Oh, we
have nothing, we have nothing.' I waited three days,
called again, and said, 'I am Mr. Levine's friend, and
he told me to call you.' They replied, 'There might be
something—come right up.' I went up and ended up
working there for about two years.

While I was in college, the same girl's mother was best
friends with Peggy Lee. And Peggy Lee wanted my
friend Wendy to work for her. Wendy said, 'I'm not
working for her. Why do I want to work for a singer?'
I said, 'I do.' So, she said, 'Well, if you want to work for
her, fine.' I ended up working for her for two years. I
try to make use of opportunities when I can.

Magda got pregnant and stopped working. Her daughter was
a beautiful child. Magda went to a party and met a woman there
who managed babies.

I said, 'I have a very pretty child. Would you be
interested?' She said, 'Well, I'm always looking for
babies.' Sure enough, she liked my daughter, signed
her up, sent her out, and my daughter got commercial
after commercial, and she's still in the business.

Three years later, when she had her son, she would take him
around, and he was getting jobs. They both are still in show business. Magda was basically a stage mother.

We were going to Mexico to do a film, we were going

*to Texas, we were going to Savannah. So that went on
till they went to college.*

*They paid for their college education through all this.
And then I said to them, 'Look, now you do what you
want, because it's awkward for me to go with you,'
and they both chose to go in that direction. So now I
had to find something for myself. I still wanted to be in
show business.*

*I joined the Finch alumni group, and in it was this
woman, Pat Addiss, who became my mentor. She
saw something in me, and she said, 'You've got to
get yourself a camera or something.' So, I get a little
camera, and she would introduce me to people, and
then she says, 'You know, you've got to get a better
camera.' I always believed in investing in myself, so I
started investing in cameras, and then, through Pat,
I met somebody who had a theater/cabaret website,
and they wanted me to do reviews. Then another
person approached me, and that's why I ended up
doing what I'm doing. So now, I'm out almost every
night reviewing, filming, or doing something. So now
we're up to the present.*

Magda was a member of the Friars before it fell apart, and
then she had to find another club. The Lambs was inexpensive.

*I found that at the Lambs, I was able to make a mark
for myself. I didn't want to be just a member. I wanted
to be doing something. At the Friars, I would put on
shows, you know, I'd put Bobby Rydell in there, I*

bought all these famous people, you know?

When I wanted to meet Bobby Rydell, I looked him up, and I wrote to his people. I got nothing, nothing. And life has a funny way of dealing with things. All of a sudden, I met this woman, and she says, 'I know Bobby.' So I met him, became friendly with him, and brought him into the Friars. I had these great shows going, and that's what I loved doing, you know?

Magda became the entertainment director at the Lambs because nobody wanted the job.

But there's a lot of problems with that, too. I'm the type of person that when you write me an email, I write back; I do things. I don't like people that don't answer or put boulders in front of you. They don't see the big picture. If it's not their way...so I have a problem with that, you know, so I'm always fighting a battle to get what I want.

Magda talks about having one of her dreams come true:

And another thing, just to go back, because I had that theater experience in Hungary, my wish in the last thirty years was if I could just connect to a Hungarian theater community. Lo and behold, through Cheryl Benton, I met this woman from Hungary who was connected. When I went back to Hungary, I had coffee with her, and she introduced me to this whole world of the top, top theater people. Matter of fact, I have one of the top directors and writers staying with me for the week, because they're doing something tonight and tomorrow night.

I was at the Friars toward the end. That's my life. I'm always at the end of something. I'm at the end of the golden age of theater; I'm at the end of even my synagogue before it falls down.

She would like to create her own club for people who love entertainment.

I wish I could find a restaurant that, on an off night, would allow me to bring in authors, and bring in music and everything, and maybe once a month, charge something. What I would like to do is have people who really love entertainment have a club where they could go, and if it's a physical club, you could go table hopping. You know everybody; everybody's there to have a good time. People who are open to great ideas, you know, where you want to learn about authors, you want to learn about celebrities, you want to learn about music and just be a very creative club where everybody supports each other, and leaves their egos at the door.

I have a close friend, Foster Hirsch, and we work a lot together. I was the one who brought him into the Lambs to interview Carol Baker, the actress, and we collaborated on a lot of stuff. We work beautifully together. Now we need the space. So, when I brought him into the Lambs, it was great, but the head person says, 'Oh, I don't know, it's too much.' I said, 'He's brilliant! Why would you put a stop to it?' We brought

*that Audrey Hepburn book there, and we didn't have
any members show up. I had to bring people from the
outside. So now he says to me, 'You can't bring people
from the outside.' That's why I want to work with
Foster to do those kinds of things.*

*There was a book written by Irving Berlin. I got the
author, and then I had a piano player that I know, and
I brought him to play some of the music in between.
You know, that's what I'm looking for.*

As busy as she is, Magda has a second career that involves traveling around the country. Since the pandemic, she's doing it on-line.

*I met a guy at a party, and he says, 'You look like the
type of person that could do a lot of things. We have a
job.' I said, 'Yes.' I would go around the country and
price things. So, for twenty-two years, and I'm still
working for them, I went around the country three
times a month to different cities to see what it costs to
live there.*

*Every time I would go, I would take a day off and
visit whatever I wanted to visit. I would visit all the
presidential libraries and stuff like that. And every
knitting store around the country—I'm a knitter.
I'm overwhelmed with wool. I can't resist wool and
knitting. I've been to almost forty-eight states, Alaska,
and Hawaii. I've done that for over twenty-two years,
just by meeting somebody at a party.*

I'm seventy-seven, so that's a lot of living I've done.

And for Magda, always open to opportunity and always creating, there's a lot yet to come.

MERRILL STONE
A Life of Resilience, Joy, and Community

*I have my twins. I adore my twins. I wanted them to be good
men, to be mensches, and they are. They're so close. We're living
in the same community, and I've got my three grandchildren
here. I'm grateful—even though my heart's always a New Yorker.*

MERRILL STONE HAS LIVED MANY lives: Broadway producer, gerontologist, singer, mother, grandmother, and community builder. Now in her seventies and mostly retired, she radiates both resilience and warmth. Her story is one of devotion to family, openness to change, and the pursuit of joy through music, theater, and human connection.

For years, Merrill thrived in the world of theater. After completing the program at the Commercial Theater Institute, she became a Broadway producer and made lifelong friendships in the industry. She was one of the first investors in 54 Below, the celebrated cabaret space in New York City, and also a producer there.

> *I was investing in different shows, which is always
> exciting. Many times, you're probably not going to get
> your investment back. But people get excited about an
> opening night, which is fabulous, and for many, that's
> enough.*

Her leadership extended beyond Broadway. As president of
a women's club in Westchester, she brought her theater friends to
perform, creating opportunities for both entertainment and community.

*Every president was different, but you could see
I was a theater person. We put on great shows.
The club served hot meals and lectures every
Tuesday—socialization, intellectual engagement, and
togetherness for seniors on fixed incomes. I believe in
that deeply.*

Eventually, Merrill shifted careers, becoming a gerontologist
specializing in dementia and Alzheimer's care. The choice, she realized, was deeply personal.

*I never really thought about why until later, and I
realized it was because of my father, who I adored. He
was this sweet, charming, brilliant guy who developed
amnesia from a brain tumor. My mother kept him at
home with hospice care, and she created as happy an
environment as possible. That example shaped me.*

Her work gave her a profound respect for older adults and
their families.

*I think I am people-driven. I love to hear their stories,
to try to make them happy, and to be helpful. As a
gerontologist, I'm dealing with their loved ones and
their adult children. For me, it's a privilege to hear
their stories and to raise the bar as much as I can.*

She often drew inspiration from her clients. One client, in particular, left a lasting impression.

*His favorite word was 'helpful.' And I thought, how
can you not love a person whose favorite word is
'helpful'?*

Music has always been central in Merrill's life. Growing up, her father filled their home with Gershwin, Irving Berlin, Rodgers and Hart, and classical music.

*He would have us lie down in the living room and feel
the music—Stravinsky, Tchaikovsky, Rachmaninoff.
To this day, I still haven't experienced anything like it.*

As a young woman, she studied voice and even performed at venues like the Fontainebleau and Eden Roc in Miami. She was asked to join Dean Martin's group in Los Angeles but returned home, homesick.

*I think that was an indication that I loved singing, but
maybe I didn't want to be a star; I was happy with
that choice. I love, love, love singing with a group.
Music brings me joy.*

Even today, she breaks into song at gatherings, around a piano, or with her theater friends.

*My theater community is complete love. It's a
great community. Communities are so important—
especially after COVID. Isolation is major as we get
older, but any kind of community—church, theater,
friends—can make all the difference.*

Merrill has weathered challenges: a difficult marriage, divorce after nearly forty years, financial strain, cancer, and sepsis. Yet she speaks of these experiences with perspective and gratitude.

I tend to forget bad things. It's part of my makeup. I remember kindness and niceties. Kindness is huge— kindness, respect, softness, gentleness. That's what makes life meaningful.

She credits her resilience to family, community, and her own outlook.

Illness hasn't been the hardest thing in my life. Loneliness and marriage were harder. But I believe in science, and I believe I'm lucky.

Her philosophy is simple but profound:

My mother's favorite word was 'goodness.' My favorite word is 'joy.' Joy, family, love, friends, kindness, humility, humanity. Life is so much better if you're open, if you celebrate, if you live a celebratory life.

Asked what she'd tell other women in their seventies, Merrill is thoughtful.

It's so subjective. Someone's best life might be different from someone else's. But I do believe we can make new friends at any stage. We can still make memories, still have adventures, still create sweet moments. Drama is for the stage—I don't need that in life. I try to avoid mean people. I treasure kindness, human touch, and connection.

She sums it up with her characteristic warmth:

Food, laughter, music, sharing, hugging—that's joy.

That's what sustains us. And if you can be a good friend, if you can come through for people as they come through for you, then you'll live a good life.

Part 5

COACHES

LYNNE COFFEY HAS HAD A long, successful coaching career. She developed principles of practice that served as the foundation for what constitutes masterful coaching. She traveled across America in a "Get Well America" tour, speaking about being kind to yourself and distributing copies of *Simply Coaching for Your Highest and Best.*

Paula Oleska's career included ballet and opera before she began her coaching career. She is internationally known for her unique Brain Upgrade coaching system.

Phyllis Campagna's role model, from early childhood, has been Amelia Earhart, and her influence is clear in Phyllis's story. She and her husband, Jerry, are now digital nomads, continuing their successful coaching practices.

Nancy Ripp White, author of *It Can Happen to You,* is a life coach, specializing in relationship coaching.

LYNN COFFEY
Life in Progress

My professional name is Lynn McIntyre Coffey. But now I just go by Lynn Coffey. I'm not as concerned about recognition as I used to be.

THAT SENTIMENT CAPTURES THE BALANCE Lynn has struck in her seventies: confidence in what she's built, and peace with what she's let go. Lynn didn't set out to be a coach—she stumbled into it while trying to understand what she was doing.

I literally was making it up, so I had to figure out how to deliver coaching in a sustainable and replicable way.

She created her own models, documenting her process as a "coaching conversation" of listening, mirroring, pathfinding, and a floodlight on the next step. She borrowed from athletic coaching—focus, skills, attitudes, habits—and built what would become foundational principles in the coaching world, including the International Coaching Federation's (ICF) core competencies.

I taught for Coach U early on. Thomas asked me to teach for him, and I said I would 'as long as I can teach my own work,' and he said, 'Go for it.' So, I did.

A lot of my DNA is in that program.

It didn't take long for her work to spread worldwide, often without her name attached.

In 2005, I went to a coaching conference for the first time in years, and ninety percent of the people there knew me, my name or my work. I had to decide whether to lean into the recognition.

Her children were nine and eleven at the time. She chose them. She felt that when she died, her gratitude would not be that she had fame and fortune—it would be that she had put her children first. Lynn raised her boys with intention, pausing her national career. But as they grew into adulthood, she turned to new ventures.

I got internal instructions to buy an RV and hit the road. I had no idea what the theme was—I just trusted I'd get it.

She did: kindness.

The 'Get Well America Tour' was about being kind and then inviting others to be kind too. But the real message? You've got to be kind to yourself first. Otherwise, your kindness won't be real.

Lynn traveled 20,000 miles in the first eight months of her tour, leaving her book *Simply Coaching for Your Highest and Best*—originally published in 1997 as *Simply Coaching*—in little libraries across the country. Later, she re-released it with a message to learn from it and then pass it on.

It's in over 20 states now. I don't sell many copies, but

*for the right person, it's a gift, way more fun than a
book signing.*

Food, healing, and community have always run parallel to
Lynn's coaching. After her sons left home, she realized she was having trouble eating properly and enrolled in a natural food chef program.

*It turned out to be perfect. I've done hands-on healing,
emotional healing—this was just another layer.*

Her younger son, Michael, even followed her into the program
and taught others how to cook simply, sustainably, and in community.

It's about joy!

During the pandemic, she gathered a small group—two new
coaches, one mid-career, and Michael—for weekly Zoom sessions.

*We went through my book, we practiced, we clarified.
My goal was to help Michael see coaching in action
and help the newbies lose their 'school script'—you
know, when all you can do is repeat what you were
taught. I want people to learn how to be with a client,
not just follow a script.*

Michael eventually realized he wanted to be a coach in the traditional sense. Lynn sees him integrating the multitude of skills he
has amassed into his life's work—helping to create sustainable communities through mindful transitions.

*I still get those 'Mom' coaching calls from both my
sons, and I love it. They have read and listened to my*

books. Chris still keeps a copy in his car. Michael said, 'Mom, I was raised with this stuff. I can't get enough of it.'

My greatest joy in life has been delivering such fine young men into the world: mannered, non-conforming, bright, well-traveled, well-educated, and most of all, well-loved. Both boys are carving out their own unique path, never afraid to take the road less traveled, even if it takes them a bit longer.

Chris and Michael both model Lynn's lifelong learning and adventurous approach with kindness, determination, and gusto! Chris, a world-class traveler, is working on becoming a Marine JAG Officer. Both boys have set their course and are putting their hearts and souls into it.

Lynn was deeply rooted in her physical community in Denver, residing in a wellness-certified building designed for clean air, good lighting, and organic gardening.

I thought I'd find like-minded people. I didn't, really— but I found people who love me, and I them. That's plenty.

She got involved in the building's governance, eventually joining the finance committee and spearheading the communications committee.

I needed to feel relevant. Now I have my calendar, my to-do list. I'm upping my game every day.

She initiated a fireside chat—residents only—to open, honest dialogue. She set ground rules: Only talk about yourself. No gossip.

And if you start getting heated, step back. It worked. It was respectful, informative, and even healing.

*And now, if there's ever a crisis, I know I could call a
meeting, and people would come. That's success.*

At seventy-plus, Lynn remains as energized as ever. Her new adventure is a second home in her small hometown, just five blocks from the house she grew up in. Ever vigilant for growth opportunities, this addition has given her the slower pace needed for deep reflection of a life well-lived, deeper connections with life-long friends, and a place to dream of new adventures as she ages with as much grace and dignity as she can muster.

*What keeps me going? Not wanting to be depressed,
or lonely, or unhealthy. I don't want to flip the switch
off.*

She's realistic, too.

*I wouldn't rule out choosing the time to go if
everything got flipped off and life became miserable.
But until then? I've got things to do.*

She offers advice for women her age who feel stuck.

*When I downsized to a two-bedroom apartment, I got
depressed. I asked myself, 'Quick—what are your three
favorite things?' Teaching, singing, cooking. Okay, I
can't teach singing—but I can join a choir— and I can
teach cooking, so I volunteered with Cooking Matters,
teaching low-income adults how to cook nutritious
meals on a budget. Soon, my energy started coming
back.*

To younger women, she says:

This isn't over. Women will take their rightful place. We're not thousands anymore—we're millions. And these young people? They're fast, they're creative, they're going to win it back tenfold.

Lynn's story is one of self-invention, faith, and fierce compassion.

You don't get a life from here on out unless you create it. So, if you're lost, go to a library magazine rack. Walk around. Let something jump out at you. Find what turns you on and then chase it with all you've got.

PAULA OLESKA
A Life of Reinvention and Courage

*Growing up under communism, the United States
was the big bad guy with awful capitalists.*

PAULA OLESKA DESCRIBES HERSELF AS a bestselling author, mindset maverick, and creator of the Brain Upgrade® Method. But her path to self-discovery and success has been anything but linear. From growing up in communist Poland to becoming a dancer, singer, entrepreneur, and teacher in the United States, Paula's life is a testament to persistence, curiosity, and reinvention.

Paula's journey began in Warsaw, Poland, where she never imagined a future in America. She initially dreamed of becoming a translator and studied English at university, specializing in American literature just because the professor who taught it was more interesting than other professors. She had no idea that decision would become helpful in the future. Along the way, she discovered her passion for other languages, including an interest in teaching English as a second language.

But another passion had already taken root in her childhood—dance. Paula's mother enrolled her in a children's dance group "so she wouldn't be a klutz," as she put it. To her mother's dismay, it sparked a lifelong love.

> *I didn't know what contemporary dance was, but when I saw a performance by the London School of Contemporary Dance, my heart said, 'This is what we should be doing.'*

Against all odds, Paula secured a passport and made her way to London for a summer dance program. She worked as a bartender to pay her way, often feeling timid but determined. That summer transformed her life. After two summers of training, she auditioned and was accepted into a one-year program at the school.

This decision to stay in London was not easy. Paula explained:

> *I grew up in a very academic environment in the Jewish intelligentsia. We were all supposed to get PhDs and work in academia.*

She also felt a duty to stay in Warsaw and care for her mother.

> *But after a long inner struggle, I realized if I didn't take this opportunity, my spirit would be completely broken.*

London became a place of growth and discovery. Paula immersed herself in dance, attended adult education classes, and even learned French. But after completing her program, family pressure pulled her back to Poland to finish her degree. Despite obstacles with passport authorities, she returned to London, only to face a crushing blow. The school decided not to accept her for another year and suggested she pursue dance in the United States instead.

With no knowledge of America, no money, and not knowing anyone there, Paula made her way to New York City.

*I fell in love with New York—and with the Upper West
Side. When I came out of the 72nd Street subway, my
heart said, 'This is where we should live.'*

She dove into the city's artistic haven, studying at the Martha
Graham School and exploring other dance forms like flamenco and
African dance. However, a serious injury during a Martha Graham
repertory class opened a path to a new passion.

*I learned a technique that immediately healed pain
and injuries, called muscle balancing. The results were
so immediate and powerful that they created a new
understanding of energy and healing. This experience
changed my life.*

Paula's enthusiasm led her to share this miraculous technique
with whoever would listen, and with a few private clients, she started to develop a practice.

*At first, I didn't even know I was building a business. I
just followed my passions.*

Over time, she became an instructor, teaching this system to
others. During that time, she also became acquainted with another
miraculous technique that used movement to optimize the brain,
and that became her new passion, eventually leading to her creating
her own method, Brain Upgrade®.

While the brain method she learned worked mostly with
learning and school issues, Paula realized that her main interest
was in emotions and changing behavior. As a result, her focus shifted to helping others unlock their potential by addressing emotional
blocks and behavioral patterns. She created a unique self-help program that does just that: the Rapid Resolution System.

After the fall of communism, Paula introduced her work to her native country, Poland, where she trained over 300 instructors and impacted thousands of lives.

Even as Paula built her practice, her creative pursuits continued. Overcoming an early rejection and discouragement in pursuing singing, she became an opera singer and performed in operas and cabaret shows in the greater New York area and even created her own one-woman show.

Later in life, she took up trapeze and arial dancing, proving that age is no barrier to trying something new.

> *When I saw a circus performance at fifty-five, my*
> *body said, 'That's what we should be doing.'*

Through all her challenges, Paula has remained resilient.

> *My mother always told me I was as stubborn as*
> *a mule—but it turns out, in grownups, it's called*
> *persistence. Even though I've made so many mistakes*
> *and wasted a lot of money, I have always stayed true*
> *to my passions and achieved my goals.*

Paula regrets that on her journey, she didn't have mentors to help her navigate a new country and a new culture. She had to overcome a great deal of self-doubt and insecurity and had to learn how to adapt to new circumstances, relying mostly on herself. Her message to others is:

> *You have enormous power within. Challenging*
> *circumstances can unlock this power—so you can also*
> *overcome your self-doubt and achieve your goals even*
> *if you don't have support. Trust your passions.*

Now in her seventies, Paula continues to inspire others

through her practice and performances. She dreams of expanding her methods and training more practitioners.

I'm just on the runway, about to take off.

Paula Oleska's story is one of courage, reinvention, and an unwavering commitment to following her passions. Through her work and life, she reminds us that it's never too late to embrace new challenges and create the life we truly want.

PHYLLIS CAMPAGNA
Dancing With Life

What the Amelia Earhart story did for me was show me a
successful example of a little girl who wasn't pretty—
and I in no way thought I was pretty.

PHYLLIS CAMPAGNA REMEMBERS THE MOMENT her world shifted. She was nine years old, reading a biography of Amelia Earhart.

What the Amelia Earhart story did for me was show
me a successful example of a little girl who wasn't
pretty—and I in no way thought I was pretty. I
had red hair and freckles all over my face, and I
just accepted: I would not marry. I would not have
children.

But Amelia—"not very pretty," and from a troubled family—did whatever she wanted to do.

Well, Susan, you might as well have hit me over the
head with a sledgehammer. If she could do that,
I could do that. Everything for me about my life
changed—and it's still true today.

From that early awakening grew a lifelong practice of turning fear into fuel.

*When I was afraid of something as a teenager—if I
was really afraid—then I knew I had to do it.*

Phyllis took diving in college despite her deep fear of water.

*I said it will not best me. I will not accept this. I will
never be a swimmer, but I will overcome this. And I
did.*

Phyllis is a woman of "magnificent obsessions"—a phrase a
friend once used to describe her—and learning jazz dancing at fifty-five was one of them.

*I am a short, dumpy little girl, but in my mind, I'm
Cyd Charisse.*

Determined to learn jazz dance after watching *The Pajama
Game*, she went to her local studio and was told that she'd first have
to study ballet.

Okay, I'll sign up. So, what do I wear?
"You're going to wear this."

It was pink tights and a black leotard.

*I said, 'I understand the kids wear this, but what am I
going to wear?'*
She said, "This is what you're wearing."
I said, "Why?"
*"Well, we need to be able to see your body, your
muscles."*
*I said, "Lady, I don't look in the mirror at my body,
my muscles. Why would you?" Susan, it was the most*

*humiliating thing to me. I showed up every damn
week."*

After the first class, the director told her that she still wasn't ready.

She asked how many beginner classes they had for the summer and rearranged her entire work schedule to attend five per week, even if most of the students were six years old.

*They all stared at me like, oh my God, who is that
person? But once class started, they didn't give a
damn. They were too busy trying to do their own
turnout.*

By the end of summer, the studio owner told her, "I've never seen anybody do this before. Ever. You've earned the right to go into jazz."

Ballet wasn't about becoming a professional dancer.

I was never going to do Swan Lake. *That wasn't the
point. The point was: Why shouldn't I do this?*

*One of my friends says that I am a person of many
magnificent obsessions. This was an obsession. That
was 'why can't I do this?' Now I also recognize I have
stumpy legs, all those things. I was never going to
do* Swan Lake, *right? It didn't matter. This would
be important— you ask what's one piece of advice
you have for women. Be yourself. Judge yourself by
yourself, not by others' viewpoints. So, my competition
in learning ballet wasn't all those fabulous people in
my class, and they were good. It was me.*

Education was another throughline.

I loved school when I was five years old, and I still do.

Though she'd started college young, she left to get married and raise a family.

At fifty, I fixed that. I finished my bachelor's. At fifty-five, I went back for more.

Eventually, she earned a doctorate—and adored the research. Her love of research extended to genealogy, a passion that once led her through cemeteries, libraries, and across the Midwest.

I became obsessed with accuracy. I wouldn't just copy someone's tree on Ancestry—I did it the hard way. And it served me well when I did my doctorate.

She even hired a guide and traced her family back to the Czech Republic, where she met distant living relatives.

For Phyllis, the opportunity to take a year off and travel around the country with her first husband was not to be missed, so the obstacles of no income, living on savings, and family disapproval faded in comparison.

We both quit our jobs. Most of our family and friends were not supportive. We were both in promising careers and they felt that we were being extraordinarily foolish to interrupt those careers in what should be our career-climbing years. We took off, and we had ... oh, my gosh, we had so many adventures.

Along the way, Phyllis and her husband were resourceful in

finding ways to finance their travels and in the face of emergencies.

In Texas, we worked a rodeo with a family. In Missouri, in the Bible Belt, we ended up helping people fix cars. We lost the engine to our van in Salina, Kansas and had to have the engine replaced. The problem was that it cut into our saved finances—we were really living on two to five dollars a day in order to travel for a year. So, we stayed with some of my family in Midland, Texas, for a month. I had done some waitressing in college, and I went into Denny's restaurant there and said, "I'm here just for the holiday, and I know your system, and I'd like to earn some money." They hired me for a month. We replaced the money and went on. John and I got to Phoenix. I believed with all my heart that the center of the universe for fun, joy, and entertainment was Las Vegas. John and I had a little bit of a spat.

I said, 'Well, why don't we leave for Las Vegas tomorrow morning?' He said, 'Well, you know, we could go to the Grand Canyon, and then in a few days, we can go to Vegas.'

I said, 'The Grand Canyon? I mean, that's like a tourist trap, right? It's like a big hole in the ground, right?'

He said, 'You know, it is one of the Seven Wonders of the Natural World, and we really should see it. I mean, we're traveling the entire country.'

Reluctantly, she agreed to take a look at it and still try to get to Vegas that night. When they got to Mather Point, she jumped out of the van.

I thought, 'Okay, we'll make short work of this.' I really was committed: I felt every fiber of my being pulling me to Las Vegas. This was one of those serendipitous moments of following my soul. I was stuttering. I said, 'Well, I don't know what we're going to do. I'm not leaving.'

Once again, serendipity kicked in, and every coincidence that could occur did. Within about three hours, they both had jobs in the park. They had made an agreement before they started traveling that they would never pick up a hitchhiker, but that day, they did pick up a hitchhiker in the park who had asked if he could have a ride to the dorms.

We said, 'Dorms? Why are there dorms here?' He said, 'Well, people work here.' We dropped him off and said, 'How did you get to work here?' He said, 'The human resources office is over there.' We walked in and they said, 'What can you do?' We said, 'We'll do anything. I'll make beds, I don't care. I just want to be here.'

Phyllis was hired into the accounting department. John, who was a very good mechanic, was hired to work on the buses. As fate would have it, John had to buy some tools, either in L.A. or in Phoenix, so they had three days in Las Vegas.

I discovered that, while it was a blast, it wasn't that much of a blast. That was another lesson.

They worked at the Grand Canyon for just about a year, and

then Phyllis was promoted from the accounts receivable department. She was sought out to become the CFO of a new multi-functional resort hotel they had purchased in the National Forest: Mokey Lodge. She wasn't needed for a few months, so she asked for a six-month sabbatical. They traveled six more months around the country, returned to the Grand Canyon, and worked there another year.

> *We left to return to Illinois when I became pregnant with my older daughter. Part of why we came home was that autoimmune disease I had. One of the considerations I had was that I probably would have had a lot of trouble with the pregnancy; there was not much medical help up in the Canyon. Our families were back in Illinois, and I felt strongly that the children belonged with family. So, we resigned. I may have been about five months pregnant. From the time we left the park to well past Flagstaff, I couldn't stop crying.*

She and her current (second) husband, Jerry, have recently embarked on what they call their "Next Grand Adventure," or NGA. They sold their home, began house-sitting across the country, and now live like locals in different communities to discover where they might eventually settle.

> *We didn't even know house-sitting was a thing, but we're beating out people with twenty applications. We've been booked solid for months.*

Though they considered going abroad, they're staying in the U.S. for now, appreciating the diversity of cultures and landscapes in their own backyard.

*One of the wonderful blessings is that we live in this
huge, beautiful country. Getting to know even our own
country is such an adventure.*

When asked why she still works, Phyllis doesn't hesitate.

*Because I'm doing what I was put on this planet to do.
I feel grateful. I feel blessed that I can make a positive
difference. And I'm still enjoying it.*

As a coach, she's often served women at critical junctures—
particularly mothers navigating career transitions. She told the story of one client, a no-nonsense financial professional, who changed
course entirely after having a baby. Phyllis had helped her create
two business plans—one if she continued working, and one if she
didn't. The woman ultimately chose the latter and later asked Phyllis a question that caught her completely off guard: "Are you an an-
gel?" "She said, 'I don't mean with wings and things, but you are,
aren't you?'" Phyllis paused.

*I was going to have a snappy comeback, but I realized
she meant it. She was in pain, overexposing herself. I
could have caused harm. So, I said, 'If I am, I haven't
been told.' But maybe, just maybe, we're all sort of
angels when we show up for why we're here.*

A recent accident left Phyllis with a broken nose, a deeply cut
face, and over fifty stitches. Her eye was saved, barely.

*Physically, I was not recognizable. I had to go silent
for over a week. I couldn't talk and breathe at the
same time.*

That enforced silence gave her time to reflect:

One-sixteenth of an inch, and I wouldn't be here. But it didn't happen. And I am here. That's how I look at everything.

Asked whether aging has changed her career plans, she said simply,

No. Maybe I have more confidence, but age isn't a factor to me in any way.

These days, Phyllis is immersed in coaching, genealogy, grandparenting, and—her latest passion—drumming.

I just want to play one of those old sixties' songs like 'Money, Money' in somebody's backyard. I want the feeling of it. Why shouldn't I do it? I just want to live until I die.

NANCY RIPP WHITE
Saying "Yes" to Life

A friend of mine wrote a book, How an Ordinary Woman Can Have an Extraordinary Life, *that really sums up who I am. My life has been extraordinary by finding the joy in the simple moments, having a positive attitude, and embracing life with a wholehearted YES!*

NANCY WAS BORN IN THE Bronx. She grew up in a time when the world was simpler, and happiness was found in a pink Spaulding ball and a skate key. Though the family didn't have material wealth, they were rich with friendships, imagination, and the sense that life was filled with possibilities.

Reflecting, she realized that she learned significant lessons in her early teens. The first is a clear memory of being eleven with three dear friends.

> *We were swinging in the park, having one of our usual conversations. This one was, how old do you wish you were? One said, 'I want to be sixteen. I want to have a sweet sixteen.' The next one said, 'I want to be eighteen, I want to go to college and move out of my house.' And the next one said, 'Oh, I want to get married. I want to be about twenty-one.' And I clearly remember saying, 'I love being eleven! I just want to be eleven.' I didn't realize it at the time, but the lesson*

there was being in the moment.

There is something magical about being in the moment. So often through my life, I remember that. I remember to get back into the present and not futureize and not look at the past. The lesson there was simply enjoying being in the moment.

The second lesson was from my father, Samuel Ripp, a true philosopher! I was twelve when he shared a piece of advice that I didn't really understand at the time, but I did as I matured. He strongly suggested not to use the words 'woulda,' 'coulda,' or 'shoulda.' He said that life was too precious to be weighed down by regrets. You make mistakes; everybody makes mistakes. The real wisdom is in learning from those moments and moving forward.

The third early lesson was from Mario Monaco, a junior high school teacher who took a liking to me. He wrote in my autograph book, 'To my favorite girl. Stay as sweet as you are, and I won't be the only one who loves you.' I so wanted to live up to the person he believed I was. His kindness and faith in me shaped the way I saw myself and influenced how I approached life. It truly had a long-lasting impact on me.

I hold these three memories dearly because they made a difference in my life at a young age, which carried me through the rest of my life.

At seventeen, she met her husband. They married when she was twenty, and she had her daughter at twenty-two. It was a good marriage, but Nancy felt she was way too young to have that be the rest of her life. After ten years, they got a painless divorce. They committed themselves to not saying one bad word about each other to their daughter. And her daughter said they both lived up to that, and how valuable it was for her. It was hard enough for her to deal with the divorce.

And then my new life started! It took on a new rhythm—faster, freer, and surprisingly fun—and, of course, filled with many challenges.

I went back to college, which I had started before we got divorced. I graduated at twenty-nine. When I went to take my graduation pictures, I was the only one dancing in the streets with all the twenty-two-year-olds who couldn't care less, really, but it was so important to me to graduate from college.

She was free to live her life. She needed a new car, so she went on a quiz show called *Jackpot* and won $4,000, which bought her a brand new 1976 yellow Datsun.

I was a big baseball fan, and I wanted to marry a baseball player. I did meet one of the Mets. That was a childhood dream, and I dated him for a while. That was thrilling.

I was an extra, with my daughter Sloane, in One

Fine Day *with George Clooney. That was a highlight of my life. He was so wonderful to everybody. I was on the* Oprah Show *with my daughter as a guest. The show was called "Mothers Finding Dates for Their Daughters." I found my daughter a date by attending a cocktail party with 300 eligible men and only twenty-five moms."*

That showed her that she could really have fun and take on adventures while still being a mother. Her next big step was joining a women's group called the Bliss Group forty years ago.

We took a stand — I am the source of life, showing up as bliss. And we took it very seriously. So, through the years, we would say, "Is this being blissful? No. You took a stand. I am the source of life showing up as bliss." And that's when my personal growth era began, and I really started taking personal growth very, very seriously.

I walked on fire with Tony Robbins, and that was a great teacher for me because it just showed me that if I was afraid of anything, I could say to myself, 'You've walked on 2,000-degree coals.' I did the Est training, which at the time was two weekends of intense learning and personal growth.

I was a volunteer on a suicide prevention line at the Marble Collegiate Church, and that was intense. That was one of the things that, looking back, made the biggest impact. We were not allowed to pick up the telephone until we passed a three-month course in

*Active Listening. I learned how much I didn't listen,
how I interrupted, and how I didn't take to heart what
people were saying. But on a suicide prevention line,
you have to really be with the person that's calling.*

Nancy had two main careers before coaching: selling advertising space for *Seventeen* and *New Woman* magazines and recruiting for art directors and copywriters. She loved both selling ad space and recruiting—anything that connected her with people, anything where she could interact, anything where she could make new friends—but it was not fulfilling, not in a deep way where she could make a difference in the lives of others.

*Then I discovered coaching. I found Thomas
Leonard—considered by many the founder of
coaching—in 1988 or '89, when he was just starting.
I found my home, my true calling! I realized I could
coach in the area that I love the most—relationships
and women's self-esteem.*

*I had a second marriage that broke my heart. I was
devastated. That's when I went on my personal
growth path. I wanted to better figure this out. I
wanted to learn as much as I could.*

*Thirty years later, I'm still coaching. I'm a certified
life coach, specializing in relationships. I really get
to make a difference. I partner with the women who
come to me, and together, as a team, we improve their
lives and relationships. It's such a blessing to do what
you love and love what you do!*

Her favorite client is someone who had a good relationship, but it's not so good anymore. She created a thirty-day relationship program where clients sign a contract to commit to the thirty-day program—no judgments, no criticism, no rolling their eyes.

I ask questions that most women give the same answer to when they're in that situation. 'What did you do when you wanted him and when you wanted to get engaged? When you got engaged, what were you like?'

I wrote my first book at seventy-six, so that in itself was quite a feat. I have always, since I was a young girl, asked people how they met. That's my first question. If I'm sitting in a restaurant, and the people next to me are a couple, I ask them how they met. They love to tell the story.

I've heard so many outrageous stories. I think the most outrageous was the woman who had a brain tumor and was given the names of three top doctors in New York. Two of the doctors didn't take her insurance, but one did. And that's the one she wound up with for ten years. After he dismissed her as a patient, they got together. Now, how outrageous is that? You have a brain tumor, and you marry the surgeon."

Her book is called *It Can Happen to You*. It was written for women who wake up in the morning and say, "There's nobody out there for me. I'm too old. I'm too fat; they all have nothing to offer me." By the end of the day, something serendipitous occurred where the women in her book met someone of significance. She interviewed probably eighty women to cut down to fifty stories of inspiration, motivation, and empowerment.

> *I was so thrilled. My friends were thrilled; my daughter was so proud of me. And then it struck. Life has its own plan. I'm on top of the world, and then the twist happened. And the twist was open-heart surgery. I had two valves replaced, and it was supposed to be a five-day hospital stay. I had so many side effects, so many other issues that popped up because of the surgery, like ulcers and sepsis, that I stayed in ICU for fifty-nine days.*

> *I was a terrible patient. My optimism, my positivity really went out the window. I was paralyzed; I could not walk. I couldn't even lift my cell phone for four of those weeks; I couldn't use the phone. I just lay in bed. I was feeling sorry for myself—not happy. I didn't want to see anyone. My daughter was my rock. She was my pit bull with all the doctors, and she got everything done, amazing, amazing.*

After two months, she was sent to rehab, still in a wheelchair, never having left her bed.

> *Rehab was quite a beautiful experience. The caregivers, from the aides to the therapists to everyone in between, were so wonderful to me. They gave me tough love. And that's when I really got to see what tough love is—it's not letting you give up on yourself.*

It took another two months to get her out of the wheelchair.

She couldn't go home until she could walk up the sixteen stairs to get to her apartment.

I didn't feel like I'd ever do it, but I learned so much about myself and about being resilient and being committed and working hard. I never exercised before. And here I was, every day, just determined not to be in a wheelchair for the rest of my life. And bonus! I lost all my hair! I lost it from all the anesthesia. I think I had four operations, and I lost all my hair. So, there I was. 'How could You do this to me?' I had enough. I couldn't walk. And I wore a wig for a year and a half.

Three years later, fully recovered, Nancy was turning eighty and thought, "Okay, let me make this something special." So, she created Project 80 on January 29th, her half-birthday. She was determined to up the ante—body, mind, and spirit.

When I was younger, I judged people in their eighties. And I was determined not to let that happen to me and to be an inspiration to others. What can I learn from other women? I went to a Facebook page called "Cool Retired Women" and posted the questions, 'What do you do to stay relevant? What do you do in body, mind, and spirit to keep yourself youthful, vital, and vibrant?' Hundreds of women wrote in with nothing that we don't know, but how much was I really putting into play? I've been living out of that ever since.

I don't know what it is yet, but I know I have something else in me. I'm open, I'm ready. But one of the simple ideas that came out of this when we went to Cheryl Benton's Renewal Summit, was a doctor of nutrition who spoke about how important it is when we awaken to move our body in bed, because our muscles fall asleep, and how important it is to drink water upon awakening because we're dehydrated. I thought, "I never want to be back in that wheelchair."

I took it to heart, and I got an accountability partner. And on Tuesday, we celebrate six months of texting each other every single day that we have done this. We've completed drinking the water and moving our body. In only five minutes into the day, we feel accomplished! Try getting an accountability partner, it really helps us keep our word!

I don't know if I want to do something around accountability. I might. What I do now with all my clients, as part of the contract we have, is I have them send me a win every night related to the relationship. And what it does for me is remind me of who I want to be, and how I want to show up as my highest self, as best I can.

I get a lot of texts, and they're all wonderful, because they catch themselves, they zip their lips, and guess what? The relationships improve.

When you asked, 'What's next for me?' my answer now is, 'Hey, I'm only 80!' There's no retirement from passion, from growth, from the pursuit of joy. I will keep saying YES to life because I know from saying YES, I'm not only creating memories for tomorrow, I'm truly living in the here and now. There is so much more to experience, to learn, to discover.

We are never too old for new beginnings! Life has a way of showering us with brand new surprises, and I'm not ready to close the door on any of them—even the new wrinkles!

Here's to LIFE!

Part 6

ENTREPRENEURS

Anne Akers is the founder and editor of *Glow Magazine* with a long history in medical publishing. In addition to her extensive charitable work, she is *The Three Tomatoes'* beauty, health, and wellness editor.

Miriam Novella, the Tea Lady, has been an entrepreneur since she was a teenager. She ran a small theater, had a bath and body store in Woodstock, where she discovered that she had a nose. That led to developing a perfume for Herb Alpert. She went on to use her knowledge to develop a line of teas and, at one point, owned the largest tea shop in New York City.

Raina Grossman's public relations career shifted when, during the pandemic, she took on the role of being the primary caretaker for her mother. Still maintaining a successful part-time career from home, she is working on her memoir.

Phyllis Haynes has a long history of ensuring that people's voices are heard. She has been in television news, structured an award-winning documentary, done cross-cultural training, and writes books, essays, and political commentary, and continues to conduct fascinating interviews.

ANNE AKERS
An Entrepreneurial Journey

*Life at home was more of a boot camp experience than
the Brady Bunch, but the lessons of discipline and hard work
would serve me well in the future.*

Born into a strict military household, that's how Anne Akers (with a wry smile) described her life at home. Her life journey is a masterclass in determination and resilience, responding to challenges and managing life's twists and turns.

In keeping with the work ethic, Anne held a part-time job through high school, earned a college scholarship, and exceeded her father's limited ambitions for her.

After completing her first year at a State Teachers College, Anne accepted a summer job for the Chief of the Legal Division of the Federal Trade Commission in Washington, D.C. Proficient as a legal secretary, she was offered a prestigious job as assistant to a former White House appointee, who had been a speech writer for Estes Kefauver. The job came with a private office and perks, but Anne quickly learned what that job was about.

*It was little more than window dressing, serving
coffee, handling files, and personal matters for the
boss. Not for me!*

An opportunity then presented itself for her to move to Honolulu, where her father was stationed at Tripler Hospital and where she would continue her studies at the University of Hawaii. During that time, love entered her life on a blind date with a young Marine F-8 jet fighter pilot, who had seen Anne's debutante photo in a local newspaper.

The romance moved quickly, and he let his parents know that he had met "the one." However, Anne was not ready for marriage, and in a tragic pre-Vietnam training exercise, the plane went down, and the wreckage was never found. That was a pivotal moment in Anne's life. It shook her faith, and for a long time, she felt numb, unable to concentrate on her studies, and lost.

> *Finding love came with joy and ended with tragedy...*
> *it was not my time for marriage, but it was my time to*
> *find out who I was and what I could do.*

Anne then threw herself into work, landing at one of Honolulu's top PR firms. When the general manager was fired, Anne was tapped to run the office, managing the team and handling political, travel, and not-for-profit accounts, including being the official PR firm for American Airlines' first non-stop flight from New York City to Honolulu.

> *Being the boss—and not serving the boss—suited*
> *me, and for the first time, I felt a sense of real*
> *empowerment.*

While in Hawaii, Anne subscribed to *The New York Times*, which she devoured.

> *New York was calling me—arts, culture, the center of*
> *business and finance. I was also fascinated by politics,*

so my mind was set, and I was determined to leave
Hawaii. Would it be Washington, DC, or New York?

Unsettled on a final destination, Anne headed to DC, where she was introduced to Daniel Inouye, State Senator of Hawaii.

As a young woman, I interviewed well, and with a PR
background and previous government service in DC,
I was offered a job as Assistant Press Secretary, more
than I had anticipated. The decision in front of me was
difficult. With no job and no connections in New York
City, the prospects were daunting. What to do?

Still, New York City called. With no job offers, Anne temped for Kelly Girls. One Sunday, feeling especially alone in a big city, and discouraged about the future, she attended Marble Collegiate Church, where Dr. Norman Vincent Peale, author of *The Power of Positive Thinking*, was speaking. His message of positivity and "you can if you think you can" resonated with Anne and propelled her forward on a path of possibility and self-determination. That eventually led to a successful career as an entrepreneur with a focus on health and wellness.

I became aware that most medical schools do not
teach the young doctor how to run a practice or other
basic business skills. This gap opened my eyes to all
the possibilities of working with this community.

Identifying a need, Anne worked with several medical practices in business development and marketing and, in some cases, helped the physicians become published authors through a boutique publishing firm, which she co-founded with a team of writers, designers, and editors. The work was rewarding, and MD Publish published many physicians nationwide.

Anne's reputation in publishing led her to be recruited by a prominent dermatologist who wanted to assist young residents in preparing for their board exams. Together, they published educational review manuals in dermatology, sponsored by an educational grant from a leading pharmaceutical company. Several years later, Anne's partner was ready to move on, and with a very favorable deal of $1.00, an agreement was reached that allowed Anne to carry on the concept independently.

Once I owned the business model and proof of concept,
I needed to find a partner who would open doors to
scale this company to a broader audience.

After much networking, Anne met Dr. John Connolly of Castle Connolly Medical, who liked the project. Contracts were drawn, and at the end of five years, 120,000 review manuals had been distributed to medical residents in fifteen different specialties. Anne sold her partnership interests in the company in 2005 for "seven figures" and reflected on the importance of team building and the satisfaction of knowing the work "made a difference."

One of the most important lessons I learned in
business is to think big and to remember that
teamwork can make the dream work.

With newfound financial resources, a longtime "itch" to launch a consumer magazine started to make some sense to Anne. Why not?

A part of me always wanted to be Helen Gurley
Brown. I saw a path to do this on my own terms, and
so GLOW Beauty, Health and Wellness Magazine *was*

born.

Anne assembled a prestigious advisory board and editorial team to focus on the latest in beauty, health, and wellness, and the magazine was devoted to "Women of Purpose." While heading *GLOW*, Anne also produced and sponsored various events to support women's empowerment, charitable causes, and health-related organizations like Tisch Center for Women's Health, American Cancer Society, and the National Osteoporosis Foundation. The magazine and Anne's work were honored by SMART CEO for entrepreneurial spirit, with a sense of giving back to the community. The work continues to this day.

Anne's career has never followed a straight line. It's important to note, though, that through it all is a connecting thread of entrepreneurship and wanting to make a difference.

> *You can have a successful career and a fulfilling*
> *personal life in non-traditional ways. I am not a*
> *college graduate. I did not have a successful marriage*
> *until age sixty. And the children and grandchildren*
> *in my life are not my own blood. But with advancing*
> *age, I can't wait to see what is around the next corner!*

At age eighty, Anne is still going strong with work, writing, publishing, events production, and a social life that includes all New York City has to offer. She has served on many boards and national committees in veterans services and women's health. She recently joined Cheryl Benton and the founders of She Angels Foundation to raise funds for grassroots not-for-profits helping women and children. And Anne still finds time for travel, including recent trips to Ireland, Israel, and a "bucket list" trip to Cape Town and South Africa for a family safari.

When I asked Anne for any advice she might have for women, her points were clear and succinct:

- Protect your health and be proactive about it.
- Have a financial plan and prepare for a rainy day.
- Get your personal affairs in order: healthcare proxy, medical directives, power of attorney, wills, and trusts.
- Maintain and develop friendships. Take a friend to lunch, make that phone call, remember birthdays, and honor the power of connections. Make others feel seen, heard, and valued.
- Find a cause you believe in and engage.
- Step out of your comfort zone: learn something new about yourself "once a year."
- Be social, be generous, be kind, be curious, be fair, and be fearless.
- Pray. Meditate. Believe. Trust.
- And don't always say "no" to dessert.

MIRIAM NOVALLE
A Life Steeped in Scent, Serendipity, and Strength

*I came out of a self-taught way of looking
at anything as possible.*

That's how Miriam Novalle describes her journey—an odyssey fueled by resilience, curiosity, and an extraordinary nose. Her instinct for fragrance and flavor has guided a life of wild pivots, bold ventures, and reinvention.

Born to Holocaust survivors who arrived in Brooklyn as tailors, Miriam absorbed early lessons in survival and hustle. By high school, she was already running her own mini cosmetics business during her after-school job at an ad agency.

I realized it wasn't so difficult doing a business.

By her late teens, Miriam owned a movie theater in the Catskills, booking local acts and hosting weekend shows. A chance encounter in Woodstock led to a life-altering friendship with legendary music manager Albert Grossman, whose clients included Bob Dylan and Jimi Hendrix.

*He asked me what I loved, and I said oils, lotions,
bubble baths. He said, 'Great idea. But you need*

training. Let's go to France.'

That one month in a perfume school in the south of France, even with the language barrier, changed everything. When she returned to Woodstock, she opened her first store, Body Sense, in 1974.

I created oils and lotions and bubble baths, and it kept growing and growing.

She opened in 1974, and Albert died in 1981. She left Woodstock because he was one of the reasons she was there, and she really didn't know what to do with her nose, "that I've now put in the business."

Then came Herb Alpert. The legendary musician heard that she was a self-taught "nose," and a record label owner invited Miriam to Los Angeles to create a fragrance. She had no idea who he was. Herb offered to fund the entire project.

He played trumpet—how rich could he be?

He told her, "You put up your nose. I'll put up the money."

About three days later, she got back home to find a Federal Express envelope with a ticket to go to Los Angeles. She called her friends, and one of them told her that Alpert owned A&M Records, but she didn't believe it.

She went to the airport and boarded her plane.

I went, 'Whoa! There's nobody on this plane.' We're
halfway there, and this man passes me by. He goes,
'I'm hitchhiking on this plane with you.' What do you
mean you're hitchhiking? 'Well, Herb got this flight,
and my daughter's sick, and I'm in the middle of
working in New York on a project, and I asked him if

*I could hitchhike on this plane. He goes 'yes,' but the
only thing I had to do was entertain you.'*

The man turned out to be Billy Crystal, who was in New York filming *When Harry Met Sally.* It wasn't until the limo took her from the airport to Alpert's mansion that she realized the scale of the opportunity.

Alpert got her a house in the Santa Monica hills. Together, they launched "Listen!," a signature fragrance developed in Paris, bottled in custom glass, and brought to life with Miriam's vision and Alpert's resources. She'd never lived like that or had that kind of money.

But success came with a price. After tensions arose, Alpert's wife cut the deal short with a massive check and a request that Miriam "disappear."

*So, I did. I packed up my things. I went back to New
York, and I was a very, very wealthy lady—a lot of
zeros. More zeros than I've ever seen. I didn't even
know they had that many zeros, and I really didn't
know what to do with my nose.*

Wealth gave her time and space to explore. She lived in Florence, Italy, painting and raising her daughter. One day, she got a call from her sister. She was marrying this Englishman, and she wanted Miriam to meet him and the family.

*The family was sitting around. The mother-in-law
is religious. She was wearing a sheitel, and they
were having afternoon tea. Now, Jewish girls don't
do afternoon tea. And there they were, having
afternoon tea with scones, Devonshire cream, jam, tea
sandwiches, and desserts, and a trolley came out with*

*tea and service and cream and milk, and I'm sitting
there like, 'Wow. This is beautiful.' We're having the
tea, and everything is beautiful. And I look at my
sister, Lola, and I said, 'Everything tastes great, but
the tea is terrible. I thought the English are supposed
to have great tea.'*

Miriam started thinking that she should put her nose in the
tea business.

She studied tea culture in Asia and discovered that Germany
had the best blending houses. She created a line of 150 teas. Back
in New York, she dreamed of a 400-square-foot boutique, but when
real estate magnate Peter Brant offered her 5,000 square feet below
the Guggenheim Soho, she said yes.

*I opened the largest tearoom in the world. In one
year, I was the most famous, craziest entrepreneur in
Manhattan.*

With 297 seats, a sushi bar, a full kitchen, 150 teas, and a cocktail menu, it became the place. She hosted weddings (including the
first lesbian wedding in New York City), worked with Bloomberg to
ban smoking in restaurants, and was crowned "The Guru of Tea" by
The New York Times.

She eventually expanded to L.A. and Chelsea Market. But just
as quickly, she shut it all down. A digital visionary warned her that
retail was dying.

I listened to some guy. I'll never do that again.

She pivoted to e-commerce, but the past few years have been
brutal.

I never thought I'd be home every night alone, eating

dinner and pulling together another bowl of pasta.

She auctioned off thirty years of her life. She didn't own a home. COVID isolated her. Orders dwindled. But she kept showing up.

I did newsletters. I let the universe know I was still alive. I kept a happy face. But if you ask me to do it again? Never. Never.

Now in her seventies, she's still in the game. A new sales team is launching her products, and she did a major chocolate show in Boston.

It was definitely a test of our ability to stay strong... Who do you want to be friends with? Who eliminated you? Who showed up?

Miriam showed up. Always has.

That memory of the pain and the hardship and $89 in your checking account will never leave us. But I'm still here.

RAINA GROSSMAN
From Achievement to Meaning

I still don't know what I want my career to be.

Raina says that with a smile. Looking back on decades of exploration, reinvention, and resilience, she has never followed a straight path. A University of Pennsylvania English major, Raina entered adulthood without a working mother as a role model.

*I didn't see women working. I guess that puts me in
the category of white privileged — though I never
thought of myself that way.*

Inspired by Gloria Steinem in college, she began to see the importance of a career and decided to market her English major by trying out different industries: advertising, marketing, publishing, and finally public relations.

By her late 20s, she'd found her stride in PR.

*It was a blend of the interviewing skills I loved from
journalism and then the selling skills I learned at the
William Morris Agency.*

She rose to a corner office, only to be downsized at sixty.

For the first time, I found it hard to get a position.
I was a generalist in a world that had become
specialized.

She turned to freelancing, partnered with a colleague for several years, and eventually shifted into an unexpected field — insurance. Today, she helps clients get out of debt and build tax-free retirement funds, while also returning to her first love: writing.
Raina is the proud mother of two adopted sons, Ari and Liam.

After nine years of infertility, I had the gift of knowing
both of their birth moms for about six weeks before
they gave birth.

Her parenting style evolved over time.

I was a very hands-on mom. My son once told me,
'Mom, if you continue the way you're going, we're not
going to have a relationship.'

That moment, she says, was a turning point.

I had to learn through therapy to have the kind of
emotionally intimate relationship I never had with my
own parents.

Today, she treasures the closeness she has with her sons.

We'll go into bed together, the three of us, watch a
movie, and cuddle. We have that physical connection I
always longed for.

In 2020, when the pandemic began, Raina visited her then

eighty-eight-year-old mother at the Jersey Shore.

We thought it would be one week. We never left.

Her brother urged her to "be a daughter" — to be there for their mother as she aged.

At first, her mother was still driving and active, but soon she began showing cracks—forgetfulness, fragility, a lack of interest in appearance.

My mother was a perfectionist, and suddenly she was saying things like, 'It's good enough.'

The decline was swift, and Raina became her mother's primary caregiver.

I had to learn, once again, to step back. My mother is the boss. What she wants, I will do—including doing nothing.

Though the role is challenging and sometimes heartbreaking, Raina sees it as a gift.

It's a magnificent opportunity to give. I'm learning compassion from it.

Now in her seventies, Raina is navigating a new stage of life.

I used to thrive on adrenaline and multitasking. Now I'm learning to focus on one task at a time.

She's working on a memoir about living with and healing from depression, hoping it will help others find answers faster and with less pain.

Her vision for the future is still unfolding.

*I want to write, maybe work in a boutique, maybe
have a dog. I want love — and to get it right this time.*

Her philosophy has shifted from striving for external achievement to seeking deeper fulfillment. As she puts it:

*I've moved from the need for achievement to the need
for meaning. I want emotional intimacy. I seek people
who can tell the truth— or who will allow me to tell
mine.*

For Raina, the journey continues—not toward a fixed goal, but toward a richer, more compassionate way of living. Since our interview, she has returned to public relations and has a client that is a nonprofit Jewish organization that creates inclusivity and advocacy for LGBTQ+ Orthodox Jews.

*You can imagine there's been much discrimination,
and so they are building community, etc. I think it tells
a good, fluid story that I'm now back to PR.*

PHYLLIS HAYNES
Amplifying Voices That Need to Be Heard

*I'm in my second childhood, so I'm writing what I feel
like writing. Instead of writing what I should write,
I sit down and write what I want to write.*

Phyllis Haynes has never stopped creating. From her early days in television news to her current work as a writer, consultant, and host of her show *Profunde TV*, she has lived with a single commitment: amplifying voices that need to be heard.

*I began doing training for Asian Americans who were
being abused in American corporations because they
weren't understood. To this day, I'm still committed to
a peaceful understanding of cross-cultural differences.*

Her academic background in Asian and Russian studies first drew her into cross-cultural consulting, long before "DEI" was a common term. She approached the work differently—healing rather than confrontational.

*Our work was viewed as less confrontational and
more healing than many of the DEI efforts that
existed, where people were shamed or made to feel
they were less than if they were white Americans.*

*I'm still committed to a peaceful understanding
of cross-cultural differences. But in the current
environment that we're in, it's just not safe to talk
about those things at this time.*

Phyllis has always been a writer.

*But my writing has been in the structure of
documentary production, for which I won a major
award from Billboard Magazine and AFI, but I've
done other documentaries and long biographies,
which require a great deal of writing. Also, news
reporting, which I did a lot of, is writing under
pressure.*

Journalism was her early calling. As a reporter, she covered
beauty and politics and pushed against barriers in an industry that
was not always welcoming. Her writing received praise but was at
times derailed by bias.

*Early in my career, I got a few interesting rejections
that stopped me from being a full-time writer. One
of the first rejections I got was a book I wrote called
The Art of the Comeback. I went to a major publisher
who said I was too young to write that book. And
then along comes Donald Trump, who wrote a book
under a similar title. And so that discouraged me
significantly.*

The second was when she was writing a great deal about the
politics of beauty.

*As a television reporter, I began to see— and I can give
you some names, like Naomi Campbell and Beverly*

*Johnson, whom I got to know. I was inspired to write
a book about the politics of beauty, and I sent in the
manuscript to Simon & Schuster.*

*Michael Korda at Simon & Schuster told me, 'You're
a fabulous writer, but what we really need is a book
on Black beauty.' I can now see that these were subtle
forms of discrimination, but I didn't understand it
then.*

Phyllis found other avenues for storytelling. Her documentaries won recognition from *Billboard Magazine* and the American Film Institute, and she continued to write essays, long-form biographies, and books. Her 2020 collection, *How to Dance in the Chaos* reflects her signature theme: resilience and reinvention.

At times, major opportunities slipped through her hands. NBC used her connections for coverage of apartheid South Africa, sending another reporter in her place but using her contacts. ABC declined to send her to Russia, despite endorsements from journalists who considered her a rising expert. The disappointments were painful, but she now sees them differently:

*I have to say thank you to ABC for not sending me
to Russia, because the Russia today is not the Russia
under Gorbachev. Who knows where I'd be if I had
gone? So, I have some gratitude that I didn't get sent.*

Phyllis's sense of possibility extends into her writing today. She has embraced self-publishing, Substack, and the tools of AI to accelerate long-shelved projects. She writes essays, political commentary, and fiction—including a series called *The Chronicles of the Crone Wars,* about older women who decide to save the world in their own way.

*My writing is just accelerated, which is what you're
seeing, and it's just beginning. I have so much writing
sitting in a vault. That's going to start to come out. I
think you even supported one of my efforts.*

She finds that her writing is also freer now, because being older, well, over seventy, she is freer to say what she wants to say.

*I'm in my second childhood, so I'm writing what I feel
like writing. Instead of writing what I should write, I
sit down and write what I want to write.*

Motherhood has also shaped her perspective. Though she
never imagined having children, she now calls her daughter her
greatest gift.

*Even her problems are fascinating. It's quite a
privilege to be a mother.*

At seventy-plus, she consults with entrepreneurs, guiding
them through uncertainty.

*My strength is helping people navigate chaos. I think
I have a particular handle on problem solving in the
time we live in.*

She believes aging offers both freedom and struggle.

*I am freer now to say what I want to say. But my
struggle is not buying into societal views of what
I'm supposed to be at this age. The voice shows up—
'you're too old for that'—and I have to sit with it. My
philosophy now is that I can start anything I want*

to start. Whether I live long enough to finish it is immaterial.

Her advice for women aging in today's uncertain world is direct:

Stop asking for permission. Trust your inner guidance system. Allow yourself to experience joy. Take what speaks to you and let go of the rest.

What sustains her is gratitude and presence. She quotes Ram Dass often: *"Be Here Now."* For Haynes, that means delighting in ordinary moments, embracing creativity, and resisting definitions of aging that feel inauthentic.

There may be people who want to sit on a porch with a glass of lemonade. That may not be me. Only do it if it's authentic for you.

Phyllis Haynes is not done creating, not done questioning, and certainly not done writing. In her words:

This is not going to be me, acting old. I take each day as a privilege. I can still run, work out, dance, and have fun—and I don't take it for granted. I take it one day at a time.

Part 7

DEFYING CATEGORIES

This is Retirement?

Greer St. John, dancer, model, and voice-over actor, simply loves working and feels that it is one of the things that keeps her alive.

Pam Ramsden's first thought after retirement was "What will I do next?" She is active in a group that helps women who need someone to get to and from medical appointments or need basic support when they are ill. Her most recent action has been, after realizing that few people in her building knew each other, to organize get-togethers for the residents.

Nancy Cook has one of the most diverse yet connected careers of all the women I interviewed. This is an excellent example of bricolage—putting diverse pieces together to create something new. She has more responsibilities in retirement than she ever had before retiring.

Joan Liman thought she was going to be a musical theater writer. She became a doctor, then a dean, then a producer, then a cancer patient, then a survivor, then a producer again, then a grandmother.

Jeannette Paladino's plan for retirement involved immersing herself fully in her new community. She volunteered for as many activities in the arts as she could and was President of the Arts Council for several years.

Jane Goldman is as busy—if not busier—in retirement. She paints, she writes, she travels. She is also active in a variety of charities, invites musicians to rehearse in her apartment, and hosts meetings of her fellow Three Tomatoes authors.

Isora Bosch, as a Black Cuban refugee, has had a long, varied career helping people. She was honored for her work with victims of the Happy Land fire, then the second-worst arson fire in the United States.

GREER ST. JOHN
Staying in the Game

I started out as a performer, acting in high school, doing soap operas like One Life to Live, *modeling—it was all that nonsense.*

It's how a lot of careers begin in New York City: with big dreams, stage lights, and a few lucky breaks. But unlike many, Greer made a radical pivot.

> *I got tired of the business and went to Wall Street. Just like that.*

Greer spent nearly thirty years in finance, working first as a broker, then in insurance at Prudential, and finally landing at the Y.M.C.A. Retirement Fund.

> *That was great fun. Seven billion dollars and about a hundred of us running it. We traveled around the country, talking to young people about saving— getting them to think ahead. That was the mission.*

After more than two decades there, Greer made another shift. She decided it was time to leave and go back to acting—voiceover work, this time. She laughed.

*I thought I could hide behind the microphone. I said,
'I'm getting older; nobody needs to see my face.' But
one of my coaches said, 'Don't do that. There's a whole
new demographic now—older women in print, on
camera, even on the runway.' And she was right.*

Greer is now part of that new wave. She's with Bella Model Agency and is featured on Herself Health, Asprey Senior Living, and Independent Health Insurance websites and tested for Forever Cosmetics.

It keeps going. I even got interviewed for Inside
Edition *with two other models about why older
women are suddenly showing up in ads. I told them,
'It's a new demographic. We've got money—whether
we made it or inherited it—and advertisers finally
figured it out.' Took them long enough!"*

She's also building a voiceover booth in her Manhattan apartment, navigating the technical challenges of recording in a noisy city.

*Even the best microphones pick up that New York
hum. It gets into everything. But I know how to deal
with it. I've learned.*

A lifelong New Yorker, Greer grew up a block from Columbus Circle. She was born at New York Hospital and raised right in the city. She went to PS 141, then Catholic school, then Professional Children's School. By the time she hit high school, they were in Inwood Gardens. Later, she moved downtown.

*This is my town. I'm in the West 50s now, just blocks
from where I had my first dance recital at Carnegie*

Hall—when I was four.

Art and culture have always been part of her life.

*I love Art Deco. I'm on the board of the Art Deco
Society. I thought they were going to ask me to do
membership, but the president said, 'No, we want you
to do presentations—because you're articulate.'*

Greer now leads virtual talks and joins preservation tours all over the city.

They're out there walking the streets, making sure buildings aren't torn down. Two of the board members helped save the interior of the Waldorf Astoria.

Greer's social life is deliberately low-key.

*I love going to the movies, listening to music, going
dancing—releasing those endorphins!*

She attends concerts by the New York Youth Symphony and supports a local dance group called Emerge.

*A friend of mine—she's like a sister; I've known her
since high school—she's involved with all of that. We
go to everything.*

She lives alone, by choice.

*I never got married. Never had kids. No siblings, no
first cousins. It's just me, and I'm okay with that.*

Her advice for women navigating their seventies and beyond is straightforward and deeply felt:

Be true to yourself. I know it sounds like a cliché, but

*it's hard to do, especially in this culture. You can get
caught up in stuff that's not really you. So, take care
of yourself—your body, your mind, your spirit. Stay
away from stress when you can. And if you're with a
man, make sure he's got your back. Without that, it's
nothing.*

Health, she says, has been a lifelong battle. She was heavy as
a kid—her mom wanted to be a dancer, and she pushed that on her.

*I lost the weight and got into performing arts schools,
but it's always been a fight.*

She takes fitness seriously and is in the gym three or four times
a week, going to jazz dance classes. She says that it keeps her sane.

Greer studied journalism and communications at City University, a deliberate choice that allowed her to audition between
classes.

*I didn't want to drop infinitives all over the place; I
wanted to write correctly—and speak correctly, too.*

Approaching seventy, Greer's still performing, still working,
still showing up. She lives in a city that's constantly changing, but
her core hasn't shifted much. She's grounded in herself, in her community of long-time friends, and in a belief that staying active—
mentally, physically, and creatively—is the key to staying alive, not
just in years, but in spirit.

PAM RAMSDEN
A Journey of Resilience, Reinvention, and Purpose

*I was so happy in my job in San Francisco, but I took a leap
and applied for a high-level position at a national church
headquarters in New York City.*

Pam Ramsden's career journey is a testament to resilience, adaptability, and a drive to find purpose, even in the face of challenges. From navigating a cross-country move to New York City to pioneering roles in human resources and clergy outplacement, and later diving into the field of positive aging, Pam has consistently demonstrated her ability to reinvent herself.

In the late 1990s, Pam faced a crossroads when her husband expressed a desire to leave San Francisco.

Despite initial hesitation, she landed the role, becoming the first woman Associate Director of her department.

It turned out to be a good fit.

For twelve years, Pam matched congregations with clergy candidates through a national database and trained executives and seminarians on the process.

On the lighter side, you could call it 'computer dating.'

However, leadership changes in the organization brought

challenges. After twenty-four years of service, Pam was abruptly let go.

It was crushing. No time to say goodbye, no time to finish projects. Just: 'Here's the door. Goodbye.'

Determined not to let the setback define her, Pam sought new opportunities. She joined ReServe, a nonprofit that places people over fifty-five in part-time roles. Initially hired temporarily to answer phones, she was soon offered a placement specialist position.

I loved matching people to jobs where both parties were happy—it gave me great satisfaction.

Pam recalls a memorable success story:

I placed a woman attorney in the City Legal Department. Years later, she sent me a card saying she was still loving the job and was so grateful for the opportunity.

However, after almost four years, Pam and six colleagues—mostly over seventy—were let go due to budget cuts.

We were replaced by two younger, full-time staffers. It was a shock, but I kept working until my last day, giving my best effort.

Shortly after leaving ReServe, Pam was approached to develop a "Positive Aging" program for older adults in New York City.

I didn't know anything about positive aging, but I thought, why not give it a shot?

The program aimed to inspire older adults through workshops, newsletters, and events.

I wanted to help others see new possibilities and stay engaged.

Pam brought on speakers, organized workshops, and created newsletters.

It was hard sometimes—finding good speakers on a limited budget wasn't easy. But the feedback from participants made it worthwhile.

After five years, Pam decided to retire at age seventy-seven, but the pandemic delayed her plans to travel and explore. Now, she's looking for her next passion project.

I want to feel excited again, to make a difference. I'm not ready to sit still.

Pam's story is one of perseverance and reinvention. From her role as a trailblazer in clergy outplacement to her time at ReServe and her work in positive aging, Pam has shown that it's never too late to pivot, learn, and grow.

Her advice for others?

Stay curious, stay engaged. Every challenge is an opportunity to learn something new.

Pam's journey continues—proof that purpose can be found at any stage of life.

NANCY COOK
Busier Than Ever in Retirement

Well, I'm seventy-six years old, and a lot of things happen in seventy-six years. That's for sure. What is very central to my life is the job that I retired from, but I didn't start it until I was fifty.

NANCY HAD BEEN A FILM editor in Hollywood, doing work that she described as demanding and stimulating. She knew, though, that it wasn't what she wanted.

> *It was just something along the way, and I finally came to the job for me.*

For years, she did custom woodwork. She had a shop in her home, and it was very arduous, very low paying. Although she loved woodworking, she found the environment dreary, being alone all day in a dirty, noisy place.

Nancy returned to her childhood memories as she contemplated a new career path. Her two sons were getting older, and she wanted to figure out what she was going to do with the rest of her life. She went to a friend who was superintendent of a school because she remembered enjoying taking her children to school.

> *I would go in when they were little, into the classrooms. And I just loved the scene in there. It was*

*alive; no matter how cold or dark it was outside, it
was alive. It was exciting. The kids were running
around. Everybody was very engaged. It was fun.*

She started to think about becoming a teacher. She was thinking about Special Ed because her father had been a Special Ed
teacher.

The Superintendent asked why she was asking about Special
Ed. Wouldn't she want to teach cabinet making?

*He referred me to a school and told me to go right
away. And the next day I went, and the superintendent
was on fire because he saw a person coming in with a
very polished portfolio and a non-traditional teacher,
which is what Massachusetts Technical Education
was, and still is, really focusing on meaning.*

A woman in a wood shop.

*So, he was excited, and he took me on a tour of the
school, and it was, to me, an epiphany. Every shop
I went into, no announcements. No one said, 'Hey,
look good because there's a visitor.' Every shop I went
into was very varied, which is also a lot of fun in a
technical school.*

*You go from a computer class to machine tech to a
wood shop, to culinary arts, or wherever the kids are
engaged. Everybody was at work, and I just thought,
oh, what an educational opportunity. I was on an
immediate turnaround.*

*This is it! And this is what I have to do. And I
embarked on that, meaning I had to go back to school,
and I had to go to graduate school on the Mass Pike at
night in the freezing rain. It was very difficult. And I
did get the job. Someone else retired, and I got the job.
So that was all very fantastic.*

*Two months later, we found that my husband had
stage 4 colon cancer, and he died seven months
later. I was new to the job, and I discovered very
quickly that the two men I was working with in this
woodshop hated me before they met me, and for the
next seventeen years, they overtly tried to undermine
my program or anything I was doing, and of course, I
needed this job desperately.*

*It was a great job for me—very stimulating.
Massachusetts students choose their shop area. They
must, by Massachusetts education law, go through
an exploratory where they sample all the shops. They
spend a few days in each before they decide what
they're going to do, and probably about 95% of the
students that came into my shop were female.*

*I was suddenly a single parent, which I never ever
expected. And then one day, I realized—several
days after he died—you're a single parent, you
know. So there was that, and you start at a very low
salary. I had two boys going to college. They both
graduated from Dartmouth with no loans. So, mission
accomplished is all I can say about that. So that job*

still is pretty central to my life because I live in a community where I walk down the street and ex-students come over to hug.

It's interesting to be a female in a wood shop when everyone expects otherwise. The other part of a school like this, in a place like this, is that it is not the place for expanded thinking. I was an outsider. Oh, and on top of everything else, I'm Jewish. I was the only Jew in the school. I'm in a school where there are no Jewish teachers. How did that happen?

And there is an academic side and a technical school. There are academic teachers. I have been to college, and I continued to get a master's degree while I was there. But technical teachers in Massachusetts only need a high school diploma, so I was an outsider. I didn't fit in from day one, and nothing improved in that regard. I certainly had friends in this school, but, yes, there was that parallel struggle that went on the whole time.

I put on blinders and forged on, because I like to get things done. I was completely engaged in the curriculum and all the work I was doing, and everything that I was adding to the curriculum, because my students spent a lot of time in the shop, and they needed other things to go to college, because we hoped that they would go to college. So, I incorporated a lot of things into the curriculum that my colleagues didn't. I got laptops in there, and my coworkers really couldn't use computers at all. So, it was total resentment. But once we had laptops, we could do research papers.

Some things just fit perfectly with woodworking as a research paper, and we did all sorts of work on computers with blogs and wikis, and all these things. So of course, the kids loved it, and it was also very stimulating for me. It was a great experiment.

I retired when I was sixty-seven, and I really had not planned to retire that young, but I had reached a livable pension wage. But that's not why I retired. My coworkers and I shared an office, and they lived in an alternate reality. They had their own spin on things that was not what was happening in the world, and I just went home and said, 'I'm done. I cannot. I can't take this anymore.'

And I told the superintendent the next day that I would leave after one more year. So, I had a year to prepare myself because I really didn't want to leave. I guess they won, right? The two men, because they were thrilled that I was leaving. But I just said, okay, this was seventeen really good years. And now I need to do something else, and I would say, by the way, it was their loss. Everything in the shop that we shared fell into disarray when I left.

I got a job doing floral arrangements at a private

school. My daughter-in-law was teaching there, and she sent me the job listing. She said, 'This is for you.' So, I went. I saw the place. I was excited, and certainly, that my daughter-in-law was willing to have me work in her place was amazing to me. You know, who would tell your mother-in-law, 'Why don't you come and take this job!'

I actually didn't know anything about floral arrangement, but I know a lot about gardening, and I'm the president of our local gardening group that takes care of the city gardens. They said you know how to design stuff as a cabinet maker, and you know about plants and flowers, and you'll figure it out. And so that's what happened. I figured that out and threw myself into it with lots of research. I did it for five years. It was great because every day was a new day to try new things, which is what propels me.

And now I'm doing floral arrangements. I have a grandson who's going to have a Bar Mitzvah in a month, and I'm doing flower arrangements for that, and I've done it for my other grandchildren. It's another lifelong hobby that I have, like woodworking. I saw on LinkedIn that I had been there for five years. I said, 'Five years of flowers—you've got to go.' But then I was into full-blown retirement.

Retirement?

Yeah, I'm imagining for everyone that takes a lot of work and a lot of reevaluating and disappointment

*and difficulty, and I sort of march off on my own.
I don't need slaps on the back or whatever; I don't
need a lot of encouragement. I provide my own
encouragement as opposed to finding people who
say you did a good job. That's what I need to hear—I
need to hear it from me—you did a good job. So right
now, I have two volunteer jobs that are together more
than full-time. But again, very stimulating, and lots of
physical activity is involved with these things.*

*And that seems to be the theme of my work. My life is
always getting up and being busy all day long. I like
that. And physical activity, and it needs some kind of
result.*

*I organized—from my synagogue—in the very
beginning of the pandemic, a local food pantry. It's
the largest one in our county. For a small community,
we deliver. We provide food for 900 people a week,
so it's a huge, crazy, totally volunteer effort. At the
beginning of the pandemic, the rabbi in my synagogue
said to me, 'What can our synagogue do, given that
our world has fallen?'*

*We talked about the food pantry, and that we could
have a whole group from the synagogue and pull
everybody into it. I said, 'I have masks from my wood
shop. I'm going to give everybody a mask until we
work this out.'*

The rabbi immediately backed out of it. He said this is too intense. We can't do it. So, I said okay, fine. Then I just went and did it anyway. I get he's upset with it. Right now, we have eighteen people from our synagogue who deliver or pack. Once we had vaccinations, I started encouraging people to do the packing job, and we work on the same day of the week, and we have a yearly get-together of just our team—the food pantry team.

There's a lot of work, and I'm on the steering committee of this food pantry and on the grant-writing group, so it's a very busy job. When you bring food to people, and they say, in whatever language, 'Thank you so much for helping me out when I need it,' that's a no-brainer.

That's it, and the people who are on this team are all retired. They all have bad backs, of course, and the weather here is stormy, and no one has ever complained, not once in two and a half years, because it's just so worth doing, and everybody feels they are accomplishing something. This is a great job as far as I'm concerned.

She's also the president of the local gardening group.

We do a huge amount in our city. And being the president was not a highly sought-after position, and it's very aggravating, and all I can think of is it's just flowers when I've got these people delivering food who never complain, you know. There are many different

*things going on in this job, and it's a lot of work, which
is great, and it's very stimulating.*

Her sons went off to college, and then they moved all over the place. And now they and their families live in the same town. Her younger son lives three houses away.

*So, this is all amazing and wonderful, and I'm
very content because I have my family, and we get
along really well. So that's a totally wonderful and
unexpected part of my life.*

JOAN LIMAN
A theater-loving physician who finally achieved her dream

I called my memoir My Limanade Life *because when life gives you lemons—well—I didn't just make lemonade.
I made Liman-ade. And I'm not kidding.*

J OAN THOUGHT SHE WAS GOING to be a musical theater writer. She became a doctor, then a dean, then a producer, then a cancer patient, then a survivor, then a producer again, then a grandmother. Talking about her "limanade" life, she says:

> *I have had some of the most lemony, sour-pucker chapters you can imagine, and I squeezed and mixed and joked and wrote parodies and survived them. How? Humor, music, theater, and the absolute refusal to waste the days I have left on earth complaining that I'm getting older. Any day I'm looking down at the grass instead of up is a good day.*

> *And I stayed myself. I stayed funny. And I stayed interested in what comes next. I have always been a reinvent-myself person, even when I didn't know it.*

She grew up in Brooklyn and attended James Madison High

School.

*Those were glorious years. I was a good student,
and I found the thing that lit me up — Sing. Think
Broadway meets high school satire. Each grade got
assigned a Broadway musical, and we'd write parody
lyrics about our school. I loved it. It was the first time
in my life I saw the direct line between what was in
my imagination and laughter. I was a ham and a
half. I still am. I like an audience. I like hearing people
react. Sing planted the seed in me that theater could
be transformational. I didn't have that vocabulary
at sixteen. Now, I can see that pattern like a perfect
traceable line. Theater was always my place.*

*Now imagine me, junior year, going to my guidance
counselor, saying, eyes bright, voice hopeful: 'I want
to be a musical theater writer.'*

But culturally, realistically, "nice Jewish girls" did not become
musical theater lyricists. They went to college and got respectable
careers. She had the grades for medicine, so that's where she headed. She chose the University at Buffalo.

*I had no idea I was picking a campus that was
basically Berkeley of the East. It was 1966 —
peak student protests, radical political ferment,
demonstrations everywhere — while I was studying.*

Later, she married and had her daughter, Melanie.

*Nobody tells girls in the '60s what postpartum
depression is. You think you're failing at motherhood.*

*I didn't know then that my mother had been
hospitalized after my birth and after my sister's birth.
She had shock therapy. But in those days, families hid
mental health history like it was nuclear codes.*

*I started getting depressed. Very depressed. It
was like being erased from the inside out. The first
hospitalization wasn't effective. The second one gave
me good medication.*

*But the pivotal moment came when my father took
me to see* My Fair Lady. *When I heard that music,
something shifted inside me. It was like a door that
had been locked in my brain, cracked open, and
sunlight came back in. I felt the depression lifting
walking out of that theater. Not cured but cracked
open enough that I could move again. Music saved my
life more than once. Sometimes musicals really are
medicine."*

That pivot led her back to medicine formally. She enrolled in
the post-baccalaureate premed program at Columbia University
School of General Studies. She got her MD at New York Medical
College and went into academic medicine, helping shape doctors,
supporting students, and mothering them academically. She used
to joke that she became a Jewish mother to 700 medical students.

Joan was working in the administrative offices of the University of Medicine and Dentistry of New Jersey. That system had
seven health profession schools then. The Dean of Education saw
something in her and asked if she knew someone to replace the
retiring Dean of Students. She said: "How about me?" In January

1994 she became Associate Dean for Student Affairs at New Jersey
Medical School.

I loved that job. I thought I'd retire from that job.
I thought they'd have to pull me out feet first.
Supporting struggling medical students — the ones
who weren't the shining academic stars — that was
the heart of the job. Ninety percent of my time was
spent lifting up the students who were struggling. And
I was good at it. I knew how to guide people through
a long, dark tunnel and hand them hope because I'd
been in tunnels myself.

At age thirty-two, Joan was told she wouldn't live beyond thirty-four.

Non-Hodgkin's lymphoma. Blood cancer. You don't
forget the smell of the room when they first say that
word. And yet, I did survive. I outlived the prognosis.

And after she recovered the first time, she promised herself
something very specific:

If I reached forty, I would give myself breast reduction
surgery. I had been extremely large busted from
adolescence, which caused major physical pain and
psychological heaviness. I had wanted that surgery
for decades. Surviving cancer gave me permission to
give myself the gift, and I did. It was one of the best
decisions of my life. I should've done it twenty years
earlier. Then, the irony—you think God has no sense of
humor?—years later, cancer again. Mastectomy. I got
my "wish" in the extreme version, but I still count the

breast reduction as one of my victories because it was the moment I said: 'If I live, I choose comfort. I choose ease.'

Now, while all this storm was swirling, the academic medicine world was shifting too. A new dean came in with a profit-era mind-set, and she was asked to step down.

I went home, stunned. But maybe because I'd already beaten death once, losing a job didn't annihilate me. It still hurt, but it didn't erase me.

I decided I would reinvent myself—again. So, I volunteered at a not-for-profit theater. I started doing clerical work, ushering, making phone calls, getting silent auction items, helping at benefits—anything they needed.

Eventually, they asked her to join the board, then to become board president. She said yes because she realized something crucial: She knew how to bring people together, motivate them, and get things done.

Her cousin, Carol Hyatt, who ran a program called the Leadership Forum, invited her to join. It was for women who were transitioning or reinventing themselves—perfect timing.

The same day, a review came out in *The New York Times* of a show she had invested in called *Little Ham*. *The Times* had adored it when it was Off Broadway, then trashed it a year later in a bigger venue. It showed her how fickle theater reviewers are and that she wanted to be on the producing/investing side of things.

At the Leadership Forum, we had to introduce ourselves—name, what we used to do, and what we

*do now—and we had to state what we wanted to do
as though we were already doing it. I stood up and
said: 'My name is Joan Lyman. I used to be dean of
students at New Jersey Medical School, and now I am
a producer.' I spoke it into existence.*

Carol pulled out her Rolodex and said, "You need to meet Michael." Michael Fraser is the guy who produced *Nunsense*, one of the longest-running Off-Broadway shows ever. Carol set up a lunch, and that opened the next chapter of her life.

*People think producing is glamorous. Mostly, it's
asking people for money.*

Joan is not comfortable asking people to invest in something where they might lose money. She learned in her producing class, "You can make a killing in theatre — but you can't make a living." So, she stayed mostly on the nonprofit side. If someone donates to a not-for-profit production, at least they get the tax write-off. That felt ethical for her. She also invested in a few commercial shows, but fundraising for nonprofit theater became a path she felt aligned with.

Her husband had trouble handling stress. When she went into chemo for the second time, he took off to Florida. He left. He could not cope. They were married for fifty years.

*Humor is one of the reasons I am alive. I write
parodies — because it helps me metabolize pain
into something I can hold. I wrote a show called* My
Limanade Life. *I wrote* Cinder Cellar — *Cinderella as
a parody to the music of* My Fair Lady. *It was part of
a theater festival. Most of my work has been staged as
readings, festivals, salons, fundraisers — some for the*

American Cancer Society.

And this was another reinvention: she was now writing her own material — not just supporting other people's shows.

*I don't like white space on my calendar. I get nervous
when it's too empty, so even in retirement, I've
been busy. Almost too busy. I've had to learn not to
overcommit.*

She and her husband bought a condo in Florida in 1999.

*Florida gave me another connection through
Avi Hoffman. He founded something called the
Yiddishkayt Initiative. His parents were Holocaust
survivors. His father survived Auschwitz, his mother
Siberian labor camps, and he grew up speaking
Yiddish first. He became an actor, and he formed this
organization to keep Yiddish culture alive—concerts,
plays, musicals, lectures. He pulled me in and asked
me to be on the board. Eventually, I said yes. And then
he needed a grant written for a Yiddishkayt festival in
Miami. He said: 'Joan — you can do this.' And I did.*

*Now this is a thread I need to explain clearly — it's
one of the most meaningful arcs of my life. Years
before, I had brought Avi the show* Signs of Life, *a
musical based on a real story — the artists imprisoned
in Theresienstadt (Terezín) — a concentration camp
where the Nazis used art and music as propaganda to
pretend they were "humane" — and yet people were
starving to death, being transported to Auschwitz,
families dying.*

The show is about creation inside atrocity — about how art kept people alive — even in hell. This show became a defining project for me.

The most haunting single sentence I ever heard in my work with Signs of Life *was this: "Only two women survived that transport." Two. Out of a whole transport. People created art inside horror, and most of them did not come back. That duality—that simultaneous grief + creativity—is a core pattern in my life too. You make beauty when the world is cruel, you make meaning when life is absurd, you make jokes in hospital rooms because crying alone isn't enough. That's my Limeade.*

People tell me they don't celebrate birthdays anymore because they don't want to be reminded of aging. I want to shake them. Celebrate every year. Celebrate every wrinkle. Celebrate every damn candle.

Try having cancer twice and being told you won't live past thirty-four—and then come back and tell me you don't want to celebrate seventy-three. Birthdays are privileges. People who think getting older is sad are not understanding the math: aging is the lucky option.

After that first grant, they needed another to fund a major curated program of Yiddish culture. I said: 'I can't write that. It's too big.' Avi said: 'You can write it. You just don't know that you can.' He was right. I wrote it—we got it—and that funding kept the initiative alive and growing. That felt like—yes— another reinvention—but also a clear moment of impact in Jewish cultural preservation. I'm proud of that.

When I don't know who I am, I write. I write parody lyrics to show tunes. I take the old musicals—the ones that saved my life in high school—and I rewrite them for my age, my losses, my humor. I would write lyrics like: "Don't cry for me, adenoma" (yes, that was one). I have a whole catalog of parody lyrics. I don't write them to get famous. I write them to stay alive. Parody is my mood-regulation technique. If I can turn sorrow into rhyme, I regain agency.

I am a connector. When I look back at every chapter— Sing, med school, dean of students, nonprofit boards, producing, grants, Yiddishkayt—one theme emerges more strongly than any "career" label: I am a connector of people and ideas. Quietly, I have changed the course of productions, careers, grants, and organizations by putting the right people in conversation. And I'm good at it.

At seventy-plus, energy is not infinite. Schedules with too much 'white space' scare me, and too much activity exhausts me. My body reminds me of limits faster than my personality does.

I don't fear death—I fear stagnation. I fear empty days with no creative spark. I fear losing purpose. I fear becoming invisible.

One of the biggest internal shifts in my later life was when I realized that my identity was not defined by having survived cancer. Because after you've survived cancer — especially twice — everyone wants that to be the headline. You get flattened into a single identity: the survivor.

But I have always wanted to say: No — I am not just a survivor. I am alive. I am creative. I am a connector. I am a woman with taste, opinions, humor, and projects. Cancer is just one chapter.

People think everything was robust and supported and fueled by confidence. It wasn't. I was lonely a lot of the time. Not isolated — I was always surrounded by people — but lonely inside them.

I had love for others — but I rarely felt held by love in return. I had purpose but not always partnership. Maybe that's why connecting others became such a mission, because I know what it feels like to not be connected. I still get lonely. I just know how to name it now. And when I name it — it doesn't swallow me as fast.

You can reinvent at any age. You don't need

permission. And even if your body is slower — your mind is not done. And even if your spouse can't hold your pain — someone else can. And even if you think you're just one small person — tiny acts can move entire stories.

I still dream of seeing one of my shows get a bigger stage — not because I need applause but because I love the alchemy of audience energy. I still want to teach — maybe creativity or resilience or narrative transformation. How to recalibrate identity. How to fail and try again. That is the skill set of a life.

Pain is a portal. I am a woman who converted adversity into art. That's it. That's the sentence. I've taken depression and made songs. I've taken cancer and made humor. I've taken loneliness and made connection. I've taken being fired and made a new career. That is the Limanade.

My life is practical and absurd. It is ordinary and extraordinary. It is art. It is medicine. It is survival. It is reinvention. It is Limanade. And I am still stirring.

JEANNETTE PALADINO
Life After New York

*I'm a lifelong New Yorker— I always thought
they'd take me out feet first.*

AFTER STARTING AS A BUSINESS reporter, Jeannette built a long and successful career in marketing and corporate communications, including positions as senior director at Citigate Communications, where she was responsible for managing the Deloitte Consulting account; senior vice president-corporate communications for Marsh & McLennan, the world's leading insurance brokerage firm; and senior vice president of Bowery Savings Bank. After she retired, Jeannette became a successful social media consultant. But by the time she was about to turn eighty, she'd made the decision to leave the city she loved. The choice wasn't impulsive.

First, the real estate market was really good for co-ops. I'd been through the ups and downs, and I knew cycles don't last forever.

She also needed to free up the equity in her apartment to help fund retirement.

I had money, but the sale would generate enough

*additional funds to feel comfortable. Selling the
apartment would make all the difference.*

The first time she put it on the market, things went badly. The broker overpriced it, the winter weather kept her from showing it well, and it sat for months.

*I took it off, thought about where I'd really want to
live, and realized I already knew—Sarasota. I'd been
visiting for years, had friends there, and loved the
cultural life.*

When she was ready to try again, Jeannette decided to skip the broker and sell the apartment herself.

*I wrote a better marketing pitch, took my own photos,
priced it just under market for a quick sale, and it sold
in a week.*

The move to Florida brought some unexpected bonuses.

*Warm weather turned out to be huge. Cold winters in
New York were getting harder.*

Sarasota surprised her with its rich cultural life: opera, symphony, theater, and museums that rival New York's.

*It's like a big buffet table, with all the big-city
amenities in a smaller, friendlier place.*

She joined the Sarasota Newcomers Club within her first year, meeting people at events and making lasting friendships. That led to joining the Welcome Club and a host of arts activities.

It's a special place. No wonder it's on so many 'best

places to retire' lists.

Volunteering became a big part of her life. She served two years as president of Arts Advocates, as well as supporting the local Sarasota Cuban Ballet School.

They train dancers who go on to major companies, and they're the nicest people.

Bridge has been a constant.

I play online every day—sometimes well, sometimes badly—but it's fun, and it keeps your brain sharp. They've done studies that show bridge and chess help cognition as you age.

She's also quick to point out that moving at this stage of life takes intention.

You can't just show up and expect things to fall into place. You have to put yourself out there, walk into a room full of strangers, and find the things you love to do. Volunteer for something you're passionate about— otherwise, it becomes a chore.

Her social network in Sarasota is now as strong as the one she left behind.

I have friends here who are like family. That's essential when your actual family lives in other states.

Jeannette admits she thought leaving New York would break her heart.

I discovered there's life after New York. You can have

a good life without being in the city."

She still visits occasionally—avoiding winter trips after one too many airline headaches—but doesn't feel the need to go as often as she once did.

I needed to be back more when I first moved. Now my life is here.

Now ninety, she knows she made the right move.

I'd like to say I had a grand plan from the age of forty, but I didn't. I was lucky—I knew where I was going, had friends waiting, and found a place that feels like home. It's been a great life here.

JANE GOLDMAN
Saying Yes to Passion

There's so much for us women to still do...

JANE SPEAKS WITH A MIX of humor, candor, and hard-earned perspective—offering a story defined by reinvention, grit, and the lifelong drive to create.

> *The premise of your book is wonderful. There's so much for us women to still do after our regular lives have ended... whether it was children growing up or careers, like mine, ending.*

Jane's first ambition was acting, but her journey began in music.

> *I took piano lessons from very, very strict teachers. At fourteen—without telling my teachers or my parents—I auditioned for the High School of Performing Arts. I just played Chopin... and to my shock, I was accepted. It was a wonderful experience, but I really had a hidden desire to move to the drama department. I tried out at one point, and I had one line*

*to read. I read it very poorly. It looked like I was never
going to go that route.*

*And ultimately, because the commute from Seagate,
Brooklyn, to 42nd Street was long and, for a young
teenager alone on trains, unsettling, my parents urged
me back to a local high school, and acting slowly
slipped away.*

Jane attended Barnard College, gravitating toward sociology. After college, she applied to the Columbia School of Social Work — "most Barnard girls in my field were trying out for that"— but wasn't accepted.

Another thread tugged quietly beneath the surface.

*One day, I found an old autograph book saying, 'What
do you want to be when you grow up?' And I had
written actress, writer, or a lawyer.*

She pivoted.

*At the last minute, I decided maybe I'll try out for law
school. I was inspired partly by my parents—both
attorneys, and my mother, one of only three women in
her law school class.*

She worked full-time for the Bureau of Child Welfare while attending law school at night.

*I was in a four-year law school program, working
with foster children in temporary care. It was intense
but meaningful.*

Graduating at a time when law firms rarely hired women,

Jane encountered direct bias.

> *One firm told me, 'You'll probably get married and have children, so we'd rather hire a man.' At that time, I totally understood their position.*

She eventually worked for a divorce attorney who hired her partly because she was a woman, then built her own practice from an office in her parents' law firm.

> *I helped mostly women getting divorces… probably one of the reasons I never got married, though I would have known how to get out of it if I wanted to. As a social worker at heart, I didn't charge much to help my women clients who had limited funds, so after a few years of my private practice, I, too, found myself with limited funds.*

A classified ad changed everything.

> *I answered an ad at Warner Communications (which later became Time Warner Inc.). They needed somebody to work full-time on a Warner antitrust case, but it was not going to be on staff. Bernie Sorkin, the father of the screenwriter and director Aaron Sorkin, hired me for the temp job. I did that work while I was still doing divorces and cases from being on panels for indigent defendants and foster care children. I was working probably fifteen-to eighteen-hour days, seven days a week, and excited to make $25,000 for the year. When that temp work was coming to an end, I happened to be on the floor when the WCI General Counsel saw me. He was looking to*

*hire a lawyer to assist in motion picture distribution
legal work. He knew I was reliable and was doing a
good job on the temp work.*

She was offered a full-time position assisting a senior attorney who was a woman, which was unusual then, handling motion picture distribution legal matters— "a job impossible to get years earlier."

For eight years, she worked on, among other cases, complex motion picture antitrust matters, racing across the country on a day's notice. Her competence and grit led to a major promotion.

*The woman I was working under decided it was time
for her to leave, and she recommended me to take
over her position as General Counsel, Vice President
of Warner Bros. Distributing Corporation. It all
sounded nice until the General Counsel at Warner
Communications said if I wanted to accept that
position, I needed to move to Los Angeles. I was one of
the few people I knew who didn't know how to drive,
so I said, 'Give me a driver, I'll go.'*

They gave her driving lessons instead. She spent four years in LA creating and then running Warner Bros. Distributing's legal department, loving the work and the studio environment but never the city. When her mother fell ill, she returned to New York and transitioned into overseeing major litigation for the parent, Time Warner, and all of its many subsidiaries, such as its music, cable, book publishing, and movie companies.

A micromanaging new General Counsel to Time Warner signaled a turning point.

I was in my fifties, financially secure, and not

willing to be micromanaged after years of working independently. And at that point, I had been nicely paid with salary and stock options, and I thought, I've worked very, very hard in my life, maybe this was time to return to my childhood passions and stop working. And I did, and it was a wonderful decision.

Jane didn't slip quietly into retirement.

I signed up for everything. I was as hardworking in my creative pursuits as I was when I was working. I immediately signed up for a writing class at the New School that led, years later, to my writing my book, titled With No Regrets: Getting Older, Face It, Live It, Love It. *I signed up for a sculpture class. I took a wonderful two-week drawing class, called* Drawing from the Right Side of the Brain, *that introduced me to painting. And then I went back to piano playing. I started taking piano lessons, writing lessons, and more art classes. I was as busy with my creative pursuits as I was with work, and I love every minute of this new life.*

In my new creative life, and when I moved to a new apartment, I began having music salons featuring some of my talented friends. The apartment has a large entertainment area that accommodates dozens of people, and I have a grand piano and a beautiful view from my terrace of the East River and Empire State Building. I just enjoy not only hearing music in my house but also providing a setting for my friends to share their talents with my guests.

She also hosts fundraisers.

It's wonderful to share music, and if it can help any
kind of organization... even better.

Once she left the corporate world, Jane traveled the world—
often impulsively, always wholeheartedly. "Anytime anybody went
anywhere, I said yes to joining them—I must have gone to Europe
five times in that first year," she says. Also, to India, Vietnam, Cuba,
to name a few places—each trip offered discovery and delight. One
of Jane's recurring themes is openness.

Be sure you say enough yeses. A yes can introduce you
to something you didn't know. Taking a drawing class
helped me discover a passion for painting. Saying yes
to trips not on my bucket list led me to discover parts
of the world I might never have seen and brought new,
interesting people into my life.

Especially now, she stays aware of time's passage.

As you get older, it's a race against time. Will I be able
to continue to play the piano, or will arthritis affect
my hands? So, my philosophy is to grab on and do as
much as you can.

For women over seventy—and anyone approaching the later
seasons of life—Jane offers profound simplicity:
- You're never too old for anything.
- The more that you do, the younger you feel
- Don't work so hard that you forget what's important to
  you.
- Better to start everything now—be sorry for the things you
  didn't do, not the things you tried.

And perhaps most of all:

*We don't even know what passions we have until we
try them.*

Jane's story is a reminder that reinvention is always possible, creativity is ageless, and saying yes—especially later in life—can open doors we never imagined.

ISORA BOSCH
A Mission to Help Others

I haven't thought about it for a long time, but I remember clearly when I was a child, I wanted to be a war journalist. I wanted to cover conflicts and wars all over the world. I have no idea why.

Isora's family left Cuba in 1962.

My father was a banker and when Castro took over, he was asked to leave the country. We started a new life in Miami, and it was not as easy as it became later. When people arrived later, they had a lot of friends and relatives. Those who left in 1961–1962, we didn't have a lot of support. It was a difficult experience. There was an Italian bakery across the street from the school. I explained to them in my bad English that I was a political exile and I was hungry. And they gave me all the leftovers every day. I had a great experience in Miami, I have to say. We were there for only eight months. I went to ninth grade, but I didn't finish.

We moved to Puerto Rico. I began to work at age sixteen. I worked at Telemundo. I worked for a cash

*register company. I was the only woman, and they
took care of me like a daughter. I stayed in Puerto
Rico for ten years. I didn't have that many friends. It
was difficult for me to get adjusted. I acted on impulse.
In less than a month, I moved to Spain. I didn't know
anyone. I didn't have admission to any school. But
when I arrived there, it was like I was home.*

As a child, she spent a lot of time alone, reading, learning to play the piano, and listening to the radio. She listened to Jamaican radio stations because she was always interested in the English language. She has no idea why she got interested in psychology when she went to college.

*I remember my father, who was always telling me,
'Well, you want to study psychology? You're going
to be poor the rest of your life.' You know, he was an
investment banker, and he believed that money was
important.*

Isora attended the University of Puerto Rico and graduated in 1969, within three years. She was always interested in foreign languages, but knew that was unrealistic if she wanted to eat. So, she minored in French and majored in psychology.

*But honestly, up to this day, I have no idea why
I chose psychology. I was totally lost and I chose
psychology. After I finished my bachelor's degree
in psychology at the University of Puerto Rico, I
worked for the Department of Labor for a while doing
vocational counseling. And then I decided to move to
Spain. I went to the University of Madrid thinking
that I was going to be a clinical psychologist.*

She discovered the industrial psychology program and it sounded very interesting because it covered so many different things, such as marketing, wage and salary administration, and personnel. She went back to Puerto Rico and found employment right away because there weren't many people with that kind of degree.

Industrial psychology is not that popular among Hispanics. So, I worked for a federal program, and I was in charge of the Wage & Salary Administration Division. And I did well. I was very successful, and I implemented a new plan. It's a field that pays good money. But then I became interested again in clinical psychology and I got a master's.

She went to Lincoln Hospital in Manhattan, where she was in the Outpatient Department for two or three years and then became the Assistant Director of a Mental Health program. From there, she moved to the NYC Department of Mental Health, where she became a consultant, then the Assistant Director of the Office of Operations, and then the Assistant Commissioner for the Bronx.

I got more and more involved in mental health and decided to get another degree in psychology. I went to Teacher's College and decided to go back to industrial psychology. I was always undecided between the management aspect of consulting and mental health. I wanted to get my doctoral degree in Organizational Psychology, but at that point, I had to work. Someone told me there was a good adult educational program. That's how I did what I never wanted to do when I was a child. I got a doctoral degree in education.

*I paid for my degree, by selling Perry Ellis. I was
working full-time, but I also made a lot of money
selling clothing.*

As Assistant Commissioner for the Bronx, she became the
principal investigator of the Happy Land fire, the second-worst arson fire in the United States.

*I helped do the family coordination for mental health
services for the victims. They made a list of the
victims, the relatives of the people who died in the fire
and wanted to match their names and addresses with
the mental health programs in their neighborhoods.
But because of this stigma that we still have regarding
mental health, that didn't work out. So, I went to a
church that was almost across the street from the
social club where the fire happened, Santo Tomas de
Aquino's Church. And when I spoke to the priest and
told him who I was and what I wanted to do, he said,
'Oh, you want me to help you look for the victims.
They're right here in my basement, and I don't know
what to do with them. I'm glad you're here.' So we
looked for people who were leaders in the community,
and they helped us provide services.*

*We rented the basement of the church, so that's
where the screening and the initial evaluations took
place because I found out that you need to identify
natural settings if you want to provide services to this
population. Most of them were Garifuna, Black people
from Honduras. And we'd also do some psychological
screening to identify the impact of the stresses that*

were caused by the fire on these people.

At the end, it paid off, but I was totally stressed out. At that point, my parents were both sick, suffering from cancer. I was taking care of the victims. I was taking care of my parents. I decided to resign. That's the year I went to China. And I didn't work for a year.

I ended up going to an interview with the Board of Education. And I got a job in District 75. I was coordinator of a program for homeless families with children in Special Ed. I signed a contract with the Board of Education that if I worked two and a half years for them, they would pay for my master's in social work. They needed Spanish-speaking social workers. So finally, I got a degree in mental health from the United States, and I got my license. And I got my LCSW.

I got a phone call that they had this program for HIV service providers. At that point, I was still involved with Union Settlement on a part-time basis. I was in charge of this HIV program, but it was mainly providing stress management. So that's why I say I've always been involved with tragedies. I was part-time Director of this Stress Management program.

After that, she got her last full-time job at Metropolitan Hospital. She wanted to return to City employment so that she could complete the pension requirement. She retired but got a call from the Institute for the Puerto Rican/Hispanic Elderly, which wanted to provide mental health services and stress management to the elderly in the Lower East Side who were affected by 9/11.

> *So that was interesting because I learned how to use music as an engagement tool with people with mental health problems, and I really enjoyed doing that.*

She also became involved in diversity training.

> *I was a Black child raised in an all-white neighborhood in Cuba, so they called me all kinds of things. They used to call me "Tutti Frutti" because I have family members of all colors. I was a victim of bullying when I was a child. It made me stronger. And it was interesting how I learned about diversity. When I went to school in Miami, I went to Robert E. Lee High School, which was in a white neighborhood. And it was the first year that it was not segregated. All the Cuban people there didn't know what was going to happen. And I have to say, it was a wonderful experience. I ended up being the teacher's pet, and I was on Honor Roll two months after I was in school. I had a lot of friends, and it was a nice experience, so you never know.*

> *And then in New York, I had the opposite experience. I was discriminated against by my brothers and sisters, by African Americans. And I learned also to accept it and understand it. It took me awhile, but now I understand it.*

Isora doesn't intend to work forever, but right now feels a duty to continue to work, in part because of the ongoing shortage of licensed Spanish-speaking therapists.

*So how can I now stay home? I was invited to lunch
by a Chinese professor at the School of Social Work at
NYU. I do some staff training for a Chinese agency.
She said she wanted me to learn Mandarin, so I'm
taking individual lessons at NYU. She told me she's
writing a grant that would bring millions of dollars
to have this project where they want to do what I'm
doing now, using like non-traditional methods to
engage Asians in mental health. And they want to
do it in centers where they have Asian and Hispanic
seniors, so she would like me to do it for the Hispanics.
And then we will compare the effect. So as you can see,
when do you think I am going to be able to retire? Do
you think that will be possible?*

*I feel very lucky, and I think that now I have to do
something with what I was able to learn. And I
also learned a lot when I left Cuba at age fourteen
as a political exile with nothing. That was a great
experience.*

Part 8

A TRIBUTE
Attention, Children, Family, and Love

INTERVIEWED FIFTY WOMEN FOR an earlier book, *Fifty Over Fifty: Wise and Wild Women Creating Wonderful Lives (And You Can Too) and* used short quotes rather than full interviews. Here, I can share two very different, yet unique stories highlighting the importance of family and attention.

Alice Aspen March's work was rooted in understanding her own childhood and early adulthood and observing her own children. I interviewed her twice, so you can see the full trajectory of her work, from mother and acclaimed weaver to advocate for attention.

Lynn Golden Meyer's loving childhood home informed her creation of a solid family core despite many obstacles. (Full disclosure, Lynn was my favorite aunt.) When she appeared at the first family gathering, my cousin and I thought she had stepped off a movie set—our very own Audrey Hepburn. Her post-college years, working in the fashion industry, living at the Barbizon, supported the myth. Her tremendous efforts to create a strong, loving family resulted in the closest bonds of any in my family.

ALICE ASPEN MARCH
The Attention Factor

JUST SHORT OF AGE NINETY-ONE, Alice Aspen March left us on November 25, 2022. Her legacy and essential work will be long remembered.

Alice grew up in a traditional family, with a father who did not like actualized women. He didn't like aggressive women. He didn't like women who showed up. She was nineteen when she got married, and at twenty-nine, as a divorced mother of two, she moved to California.

> *I found another guy to marry in June of '63, May of*
> *'63. So now I had his son—he was a widower. I had*
> *three boys: a stepson and my two boys. And I was still*
> *a mother. And then I got pregnant and had another*
> *son.*

She became an award-winning weaver and loved it. Her life changed when her son, Mark, called her up and said, "Alice, I'd like you to give a lunch for the Media Reform people in Los Angeles.

And I'll pay you."

This was the beginning of her connection to children's television. She became involved in keeping Mr. Rogers on the air and continued to focus on the impact of television on children.

I would not be ninety if I had not discovered what my work is. It makes such a difference all over—the fact that when you get the kind of attention you need, you thrive. Now, the more I do this work, the more I realize the healing that we're doing. It all comes from the inside, anyway. You can't get anybody else to heal you. You have to really feel.

I spent four and a half years learning everything I could about the impact of TV viewing on children. I started a group called FACT—Focusing Awareness on Children and Television. I spoke all over California because people were eager to hear. I had some deep throats who were in careers in television, and one of them called me up one day and said, 'You've got to do something. KCET is not going to buy Mr. Rogers.' I said, 'OK.' At that time, I was on the Community Advisory Board of KCET, which was an appointed position.

I wrote them a letter on our stationery, and I said, 'OK. If you're not going to buy Mr. Rogers, who are you going to buy for that age group?' And they had nobody else. So, they had to buy Fred Rogers, which kept him on the air for twenty-five years.

She discovered that the secret is feelings that we never had and don't know how to deal with. The "Attention Factor" is the bearer of feelings. The root cause.

> *I've said for years, our behavior and the kind of attention we get is the root cause of our behavior and our feelings.*

Alice went to Japan in September of 1953, when she was twenty-one.

> *I got my Japanese soul. I realize now that my nine months in Japan with this family were the most important nine months of my life. They gave me what I needed, these strangers, and they live in my heart. My parents, unfortunately, didn't know a thing about attention. They never had the kind they needed, and if you don't get it, you don't know what it means, and you can't give it to anybody else.*

She wrote her first book in Los Angeles and self-published it in 1995.

> *Attention is much more than a word. It's our primary need. It is everyone's issue. It can be a life-or-death matter. We love it. We'll kill for it, and sometimes we die for it. It gives me a lot of power to know that I can change people. I just say how are you, how's your day going? And if they smile, I know that I've given them the kind of attention they need, because it's not where it's just something our body does, it just feels good.*

When she was seventy-seven years old, she moved to New York. She knew that coming here would give her a bigger platform. She spoke 24/7 in Los Angeles.

I was everywhere. I was in the Congressional Record *when I started talking about the impact of TV viewing on children and families. I hated television because it told us what to do, and it was outside telling us more that we didn't know anything. I watched a lot of really good programs, and the commercials would come on and tell me to go to the kitchen or go to the store and buy some kind of toilet paper. I didn't like that at all.*

And then my kids were growing up. It was different when they were born, and I sat in front of the television set watching when they were seven and eight. I sat with them and watched. Mark was in Washington, DC when he was twelve years old, working for senators. I asked him one day if he'd like to go to the Burbank Airport and meet a potential president, and he said, sure. I asked him that question, but he ended up working for Birch Bayh in the Library of Congress and the Senator from Minnesota.

I became a zealot, and I said, 'I've got to do something about this.' This is even before I moved to New York, but I was already talking about it. I was starting a group, and we had a membership of 125 people. Everywhere they wanted me to go, I would. I could talk 24/7. Nobody sounded like I did, and that was at the very beginning.

I hadn't really learned about attention when I first moved to New York. And then somebody else used the word "attention," and I had an epiphany— one word over my head in dimensional letters, the word ATTENTION! That's a strange, wonderful thing. I don't know where that came from."

She started doing workshops, and there was a second edition of her book in 1995. She wrote another book that was geared more towards college students. She wrote about visiting your teachers, who put a sign on the door— "My office hours are from what to what; please come"— but kids never do.

I talked about that the other night because I had a guest here who was teaching college, and nobody comes to see him. I said, 'That's a waste, isn't it?' He said, 'Absolutely.' So those are the things I talked about.

My energy, Susan, comes from the fact that I'm making a difference in people's lives. And in a strange, bizarre way, this lockdown, as lethargic as it has made me, has been good for me, because I learn things.

Attention. It's your most powerful personal tool. I had to learn all of this. It's come through my relationships. They're the most important part of your life. Make them a priority. They change your life and put you on the fast track to success.

A lot of people don't even know what I meant—that to arrange independent living on your own makes you accountable. So, with responsible vision, every action or choice you make creates your future.

*I was currently writing this book to myself, but there's
a line that volunteering gives you an experience of
making your world a better place.*

I knew Alice was doing workshops, and then she started a radio show.

*Yeah, I did. I have interviewed over a hundred people.
I didn't realize I knew that many—I mean, I've only
been here fourteen years.*

Alice had a big following with the radio show. She won a prestigious contest and had a billboard in Times Square.

*But why am I still doing this? Because it's so simple,
but it really looks like we never learned that when
people get the kind of attention they need, they smile.
I've had CEOs write to tell me we never saw our group
so energized. I've used your steps with my older adult
kids, with whom I had no relationship. It changed
the relationship. The testimonials I get are absolutely
amazing.*

*So, as bad as the lockdown has been, my most
important learning has been that it could be bad and
I could survive. I belong to a group, and I stopped
participating in the group. I just didn't want to
anymore. There were only five of us. All the rest were
very interesting. I just discovered I was the only non-
PhD. There's an article in something I read recently*

where it said that the drive for PhDs in this country is absolutely the root cause of our changing the whole college system, and the people who go to college.

The last time I talked at NYU Langone Hospital, (I always watch somebody in the room to see if they're getting it), this young man, he had to be early thirties or very late twenties, was writing so fast I was amazed. He just wrote, wrote, wrote, and then he left when it was over. But he came back, as I was walking out, and I stopped, and said, 'You were a fabulous audience member,' and he just looked at me, and said, 'I learned so much.'

When I leave, the final remark that is made by the audience is, 'Why haven't we learned this before?' It changes lives. It changed my life. So, I guess that's why I continue to do it. I can see results.

I did it by the seat of my pants, because that's who I am. I've been on several important committees in New York and in California, including the California State Senate on the future of public broadcasting. But you know, I think I keep going because I have been empowered. I empower others. That gives me energy, you know."

Alice's advice for women of a certain age who are feeling invisible and washed up and think they have nothing left to give:

Well, I think that my work plays a role in this because,

as an older person, you have to own who you are. People come up to me all the time—they've been doing this for several years now—and say, 'I want to be like you when I grow up.' I used to say, 'Thank you.' I don't anymore. I say, 'Well, don't you want to know how I got there?'

That's growth on my part, because I want to hook them in, because when you know how to take care of yourself, when you know what you genuinely need, you don't have to feel that you don't make a difference. It makes a difference because if you know about attention, you can't not use it. You just can't because we can see attention. We can hear attention.

LYNN GOLDEN MEYER
Entrepreneur and Matriarch

*Lynn Golden Meyer passed away on March 23, 2023,
at the age of 87.*

LYNN TALKED ABOUT HOW SHE found her way to New York City and into the fashion industry.

*I knew that I wanted to go away to school, which is
not what all my girlfriends did. I went off to Elmira,
which was a girls' school in upstate New York, for
just about two years, and then I had to leave—I was
expelled. And then I went to school in New York City,
which was basically what I had wanted to do anyway.
I wanted to work in fashion—not designing it but
working with people in the fashion industry.*

*And that's basically what I learned. The school I went
to was called The Tobé-Coburn School for Fashion
Careers. It was a division of Barnard College. It was a
good school, and I finished my fourth year there. And I
lived in a hotel—the Barbizon Hotel, which was a hotel
for women at the time. But it didn't stop us—most of*

the girls at the school were living there, and I stayed
on after I graduated."

Lynn described the Barbizon years as working by day and spending many evenings at the Copa with wealthy, eligible young men.

She worked in a catalog house—doing what they call merchandising—getting models set up for the shoes for the pictures, rather than fitting the clothes on them and adding accessories—so this was a fun job. She met all the models of the day. This was what they called catalog work, and it was their bread and butter. They earned good salaries, and this is what kept them in their fancy clothes.

Those were the days when you could buy clothes at
Sears Roebuck, J.C. Penney, Montgomery Ward,
and they all had catalogs, thick, thick catalogs with
the fashions of the day. You didn't have the shopping
centers to go to as easily. It's a little like going online if
you don't want to go to the mall.

She was working in the housewares department at Bloomingdale's when she met her future husband, George. She was in the bath shop, and he was in the kitchen shop, and employees weren't allowed to fraternize, so they would meet at the elevators and talk so they could hide. He was living in Brooklyn, and she was living in Manhattan, so it was a long trip to date her, but he did it.

Lynn and George had a double wedding with her sister. They went to Miami for their honeymoon, and then on to Havana as Castro's troops were coming in.

"We saw them marching down the streets. It was very,
very interesting. I mean, it never interfered with our
vacation, our honeymoon. I guess we stayed there

*about a week, and then we came home. And shortly
after that, I became pregnant, so that's when I went to
work for* Parents' Magazine. *I worked there up until I
was ready to give birth."*

She worked for *Parents' Magazine* in the fashion photography department. She worked with the child models, picking out the clothing for them to wear and making sure that the photographer did a good job and that the kids did what they were supposed to do without interference from their mothers.

George was still working at Bloomingdale's when she gave birth to her daughter, Melinda.

*I was twenty-five years old when Melinda was born.
My mother was twenty-five when I was born. And ten
and a half months later, Josh was born. And exactly
twelve months later, Diana was born. So, we had
loads of fun. We didn't have plans to have children so
quickly, and certainly not as fast as I did. People used
to joke and say I must have conceived while I was still
in the hospital with the last one.*

They moved several times before settling in Framingham, where David was born. Lynn began to work with George at Trade Centers. This was full of salesmen—the clothing salesmen and the gift salesmen. She worked with him there, never on the road, but in the showroom, and learned a great deal.

*Once I divorced him, I went to work for another rep
as a showroom rep, and then I worked for another rep
after that. I was working on my own at that point and
earning a salary. It wasn't much, but it was a salary.
And here I am after forty years, still very happy and*

not willing to give up my house.

Working in the showrooms was great. There were lots of different people, which I love. The people who came to the showrooms were store owners or buyers, mostly from the East, from north of New York. So, it was mostly New England that came in, and then we had trade shows throughout New England a few times a year. You met lots of different people and told them how much to buy, what to buy, and how to get out of their mistakes without insulting them.

She was always on the road. She would come home at the end of the week and cry sometimes because she was so glad to be home.

Everybody thought I was making so much money, but half of it was going to my expenses. Hotels and restaurants are not cheap.

I broke my arm, and I couldn't drive, so since I couldn't bring in business, I resigned. So here I am now, retired. I plan on going to Africa sometime next winter with Josh. I have always wanted to go to South Africa—always. I adore the music, the color, everything about it. I said to myself, 'What the hell? I might as well cash in a CD and do something I've always wanted to do. So, I am going to South Africa.

Along the way, Lynn faced several major challenges.

I had lung cancer. I had half a lung removed and went back to work. Three of the kids were in college at the same time; I had to work. I had to help these kids out. Luckily, they were all good students, so they all got scholarship money as well as financial aid. Friends helped out, and everybody was a big help when that happened. And I wasn't laid up for that long. I remember being in the hospital for about three weeks, and when I came home, my mother and my sister came to stay with me, and all was well.

"A lot of things were a challenge. A friend said to me, 'I don't know how you do it," and the only answer is that you don't have a choice. Many things are a challenge, but you just work through them; you have to overcome them or find a way to get around them. There's no choice; you can't give up. I had to get rid of my husband because he was not the kind of man I wanted to be around, to put it mildly. He was a challenge. At that point, no one got along with him. But the divorce was messy, and being in court with him all the time was messy. He fought with his own lawyer—punched him out.

I was working with a customer in Vermont one day, and I got a phone call telling me they discovered that David had a tumor. David had cancer. I cried, I cried, I cried; I don't think I ever cried so hard in my life. I managed to drive myself home. David started going through chemo and radiation all at the same time, daily. It wasn't just once a week; it was every day. He lost all his hair and everything.

*At the time, David was living with his girlfriend,
Annalisa. They had known each other for years and
were totally devoted to each other, so she was with
him. I went down to DC and spent some time there. It
was hard to sit with him as he went through radiation.
And Josh, his older brother, told his boss at work, "I'm
taking my brother in every morning, and I'm taking
him home whenever he's finished. My work will get
done."*

*Just as he finished with his chemo, he and Annalisa got
married. It was a beautiful wedding. David was bald,
and all his groomsmen and best man were bald. They
all shaved their heads in honor of David's baldness. It
was a nice tribute to David.*

*He had another tumor removed a couple of years
later, from his back, and hopefully, they got all of
it. And then just a year ago, he had a brain tumor
removed. He had the tumor removed just after Sadie
was born.*

Her children were close to her and to her parents as they grew
up, and they are still close to her now.

*They're sensible kids, and I hope that I instilled a lot of
good things in them. The early years with their father
were happy. They're good kids; they've got brains,
they've got feelings, they've got empathy, sympathy. I
don't know how else to describe it. I love them dearly,
and they all love each other dearly... and me.*

*I'm satisfied with my life. I'm unhappy about the
wrinkles on my face, and I'm unhappy about little
things, physical things like my weight, that sort of
stuff, but all in all, I would say life is good. If I had
more money, life would be much better, but that's
the way it is, and I'm going to have to get through it
this way. If I have to be a bag lady, I will. I can stay
mentally healthy enough to last as long as my money
does.*

*How can you give up? You can't give up! Now I have
a house to maintain. I can't give up on it unless I'm
ready to move, and I don't want to move. I have
children who look up to me and want me around them,
and I can't give up for that reason. There are some
people who give up the things that caused them grief
or pain without another thought, but no, I wouldn't
give up anything for the way things are.*

SOME FINAL THOUGHTS
How to Remain Effervescent

ONE ASPECT OF GROWTH AND change that has not been discussed earlier in the book is transformation and transformative learning. Some women follow a fairly straight path, while others come to a place where their life doesn't make sense—there is a sudden jolt—and a process leads them to a different path.

This process of rethinking and changing is called transformative learning. When a significant change in thinking results in behavioral change, it is called perspective transformation (Mezirow, 1991). One's whole way of thinking about the world changes through shifts in the thought patterns that lead to decisions and behavior. Following is a formal look at the process:

The Six Steps of Transformative Learning

1. **Experiencing a disorienting dilemma.** At some point, the individual realizes that what they are doing is somehow out of sync with the rest of the world. It's the jolt of discovering your view of the world is different from that of others or that

the world has thrown you a curveball. This could be losing a job, getting divorced, or simply finding yourself in a situation that is not what you had thought it would be.

2. **Undergoing self-examination.** After discovering a disconnect, the individual moves into a period of looking at what they are doing and believing. It often involves moving from the notion that something must be wrong with you—and therefore, you should just accept what is happening in your life—to beginning to wonder if there's really something wrong outside of yourself.

3. **Conducting a critical assessment of role assumptions.** This next step involves looking at how you are functioning and examining the assumptions or deeply held beliefs underlying how you are living your life, looking at what you have been led to accept.

   Examples:
   - All widows must withdraw from the world, wear black, and never be happy again.
   - All mothers must stay home with their children.
   - People who accept public assistance will never go off it.

   The key question here is, to quote Byron Katie, "Is that really true?"

4. **Recognizing that one's problem is shared.** Sometimes, if you are out of sync with the norms that are familiar to you, it is easy to think that you are all alone. It becomes easier to change when you realize that you are not alone.

5. **Exploring options for new ways of acting.** You begin to generate alternatives and plans, based on your revised assumptions about yourself and the world.

6. **Building competence and self-confidence in new roles.** Finally, the individual proceeds with changed behavior. Long-held habits of mind or perspective are examined, resulting in the creation of new or altered perspectives. In order for this process to be transformative, both thinking and subsequent behavior must change. A big part of transformative change or perspective transformation, then, goes beyond recognizing triggers to reflection—thinking about an old behavior pattern, deciding whether to keep the pattern or change it, and, if changing, experimenting with changing that pattern.

This process of self-reflection has been thoroughly documented on the individual level: the beliefs that people hold about themselves are key elements in determining how they will act. We set up filters based on what we believe to be true and act in ways that are consistent with those filters—unless something turns our lives around (Mezirow, 1991).

A few examples of disorienting dilemmas are:

At the same time, she was shopping for Unitarian Churches in the City. Deb Roth walked into 4th U and never left. It was there that she was introduced to the whole notion of the Divine Feminine, and for her,

"That just cracked things open. It's like, Oh, my God! This is what has been missing in my own personal connection to the divine—this whole notion of the goddess."

It wasn't until years later, while talking with other mothers, that Rita Battat recognized subtle patterns in how grief and loss shape family dynamics.

"All of a sudden, it hit me—a little light bulb went off. That's how this *started*."

Nancy Cook had been a film editor in Hollywood, doing work that she described as demanding and stimulating. She knew, though, that it wasn't what she wanted.

"They were just something along the way, and I finally came to the job for *me*."

Attitude

Attitude is a strong factor in resilience. Many of the women described their positive attitude:

"Every morning, I write down three things I'm grateful for. It changes your energy. You start to look for the *good*."

~ *Donna Karlin*

"My oncologist said it wasn't possible. I said, 'Just watch me.' And he did. I've been given this life—so I'll do something with it. I want to live a meaningful, joyful life. One with purpose."

~ *Minx Boren*

"It's about staying in the game of life. Never, ever giving up."

~*Beatty Cohan*

"It's very important to wake up with a smile on your face and a sense of purpose. I feel we must have passion, compassion and enthusiasm for living and be grateful for every day that we remain healthy on this planet!"

~ *Randie Levine Miller*

"I came out of a self-taught way of looking at anything as possible."

~*Miriam Novalle*

"Be true to yourself. I know it sounds like a cliché, but it's hard to do, especially in this culture. You can get caught up in stuff that's not really you. So, take care of yourself—your body, your mind, your spirit. Stay away from stress when you can. And if you're with a man, make sure he's got your back. Without that, it's nothing."

"Stay curious, stay engaged. Every challenge is an opportunity to learn something new."

~ Pam Ramsden

"Your girlfriends are the ones who keep you going. It's important to have good friends—and to be one."

~ Pat Addiss

A Checklist for Effervescence

Take care of yourself

Have regular check-ups. Go beyond just seeing your PCP and the obvious (mammogram, vision, teeth) to periodically see all the specialists you might need. Those of us who spent our summers on the beach should have at least one full-body scan to be sure that sun damage isn't showing up. Feel like you aren't hearing well? Research is finding a relationship between hearing loss and suspected dementia.

Cultivate and retain friendships

Lack of human contact can easily lead to depression. Your inner circle can be strong and small – a few people that you are in contact with somewhere between daily and weekly. Around that core, you might have several groups based on common interests – movies, theaters, food, knitting, singing, spiritual activities, volunteering, traveling. Anything that brings you together with other people provides excitement and sometimes surprises. Do keep track, though. At one point, I discovered that I was part of about ten groups, some overlapping. As an introvert, instead of giving me warm feelings, it turned out to be a source of stress, and I had to cut back to half that number. It may take a bit of time to discover what works for you.

Try new things

Experiment. Be curious. Try something new. This could be as simple as changing your route to discover a new neighborhood. I know women who have tried everything from parachute jumping, going on solo trips, and taking ballet classes to those who tried different restaurants, studied yoga, and took an improv class. Curiosity and exploration keep us young, interesting, and vibrant.

Keep thinking

Do crossword puzzles (the mini is fine), Sudoku, Wordle. Take an online language class. Go to museums, theaters, and lectures.

Stay open to new things and possibilities.

A woman who started as a math teacher moved into marketing, allowing her to live in other countries. She then became an artist, a coach to artists, a real estate agent and taught healthy cooking before moving to Maine to become a disc jockey.

Smile!

Smiling opens up your face and raises your spirits. Smiling is contagious—you're creating a nicer world.

Love

Love people. Allow people to love you. Make your home and workspace places you love. Create an environment of generosity and kindness.

Think young

Too many women moan and groan about getting older. As my endocrinologist used to say, "Consider the alternative." There are so many vibrant, effervescent women over 90 out there celebrating every minute of their lives. One ninety-year-old cabaret singer still does a few numbers perched atop a piano. Champagne Ladies run marathons, write books, teach yoga classes, paint, act—the possibilities are endless.

ACKNOWLEDGMENTS

It took a tribe to bring this book into existence. That tribe includes every woman over fifty, most of whom I have yet to meet, who embody the principles in this book—the countless women who took a stand against ageism, sexism, appearance-ism, and all the forces that try to diminish us, to limit us, and try to make us invisible. I may never meet you, but nonetheless, am deeply in debt to you.

Thank you to the thirty-eight women who took the time to tell me their stories, to review them, and allowed me to create the wonderful profiles in this book. They patiently worked through long interviews, corrections, and revisions. I also honor and respect the small number who decided that they didn't want to be included.

The Three Tomatoes Publishing has created an incredible space for authors, and I'm proud that this is my second book with them. Cheryl Benton is a joy to work with. She is involved in every step of the process and provides all the support an author often only dreams of. She was a big part of my decision to stick with this project. This would not have happened without her.

My personal support team has seen me through dry spots, lack of faith, threats of quitting, and hating my writing, at every stage of the project. They have been my cheerleaders, my consolers, and my task masters. Thank you, Betsy Mickel, Susan Forster, and Patricia Neil.

Stephanie Raffelock was my champion in the first writing group I joined and has continued to support my writing and to encourage me along the way. Amy Ferris, thank you for telling me that I could do this! Vera Andersen, another writing group partner who became very dear to me, thank you for all your support and friendship.

Thank you, The Three Tomatoes authors' group, especially Robin Lieberman. Thank you, Jane Goldman, for hosting the group.

Thank you, Bonnie Edner and Javier Medina, my neighbors who have supported me through all manner of household dramas, including cat sitting, and have become family to me in the years they've lived one flight down.

Finally, thank you to my mother, whose diaries inspired me to write.

ABOUT THE AUTHOR

DR. SUSAN R. MEYER HELPS people create the life they want and
has spent decades working with women and men who want to
create a clear path to success. Whether you're looking for a totally
different path or simply want to tweak your life, her extensive experience in life, career, and transition coaching will help you take an
informed look at your own life and build on what's revealed. Susan
brings an eclectic background to her practice. Her skills in getting to
the heart of issues and working with clients to craft clear plans grew
out of years of coaching, teaching (pre-school through grad school)
and training (trainers and line staff through executive managers).

Her curiosity and her coaching experiences fed into her
passion for interviewing women and sharing their stories. Her
book, *Fifty Over Fifty: Wise and Wild Women Creating Wonderful
Lives (And You Can Too!)* tells the stories of fifty amazing women
who have created exciting life paths and served as a springboard for
this book.

Susan's background includes decades of creating innovative programs that enabled managers to excel as leaders. Her personal growth workshop, Women Living for Today and Tomorrow, was featured in *The New York Times*. Unwilling servant of two rescue cats, she still finds time to travel and enjoy theater, movies and events with friends. Follow her at Champagne Ladies at the Life-Work Cafe on substack.com or visit her website: www.susanrmeyer.com

www.ingramcontent.com/pod-product-compliance
Lightning Source LLC
Chambersburg PA
CBHW051505150726

47997CB00001B/120